IMM
Modeling Method
Business Procedure
Modeling

11th Edition

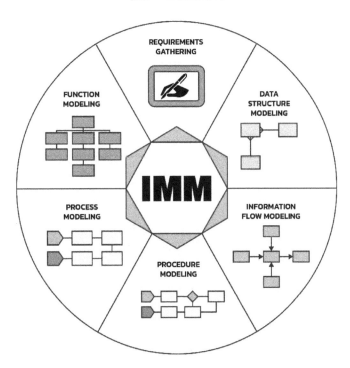

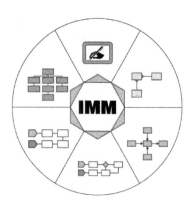

Table of Contents

1. I

Welcome to
suite of boc

1.1. T

Introducing
business an
full potenti:
of dedicate
empower y
tangible bu

IMM stand:
from a dive
of incredibl

IMM's miss
integrated,
accuracy ar
avoiding th

Say goodby
efficient spi
blend of sp
enterprise 1

Using the II
rewarding e
offers.

1.2. T

IMM provic
maximize a
of these ar

Requirem
Gathering

Business F
Architectu

17.1?

18.

19.

20.

21.

Data Architecture Modeling	This is the technique used to identify and model the elements of data, and the way in which these elements are related to each other, so an *Enterprise* can create the INFORMATION it requires to effectively execute its Business Functions. The *Data Architecture Model* is the cornerstone to success for all *data quality*, *data governance*, *master data management* and *database development* projects.	
Business Process Modeling	This is the technique to use when you need to know and model the precise order in which the Business Functions need to be carried out in response to a triggering event and arrive at a predefined and desirable business outcome. For example, "what steps must the enterprise take, and in what order, to register a new customer and issue their first bill?"	
Procedure Modeling	This is the technique to use when you need to *know and show* HOW *Business Processes* ought to be implemented on a day-to-day business using existing technologies and standards.	
Information Flow Modeling	This is the technique to use when you need to know and show how information flows into, around and out of the Enterprise.	

Each of the architecture models in IMM is built based on elements from the Business Function Architecture. Because of this, all the models are fully integrated, which provides a richness, rigor and consistency that is not currently offered by any other business architecture modeling method.

2.   What is Business Procedure?

To truly understand Business Procedure, we must first understand two other fundamental business elements, Business Functions and Business Processes.

2.1. Business Function

These are the core activities that an enterprise must perform in order to meet its business objectives and continue in existence. Business Functions are a definition of *what* it is the enterprise *ought* to be doing.

From this definition, it can be seen that Business Functions are pretty important things. All other business elements, such as Business Processes, Business Procedures and Data are derived from the Business Functions of the enterprise.

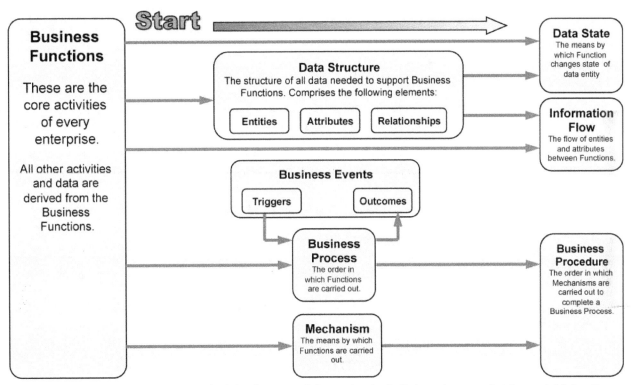

Diagram showing the sequence in which business models need to be built in order to maintain model integrity.

2.2. Business Mechanisms

Normally called a Business Mechanism, this is the *means* by which a Business Function may be performed under particular circumstances.

2.3. Business Process

Business Functions define *what* an enterprise *ought* to be doing. Business Processes define the *order* in which this ought to be done.

2.4. Business Procedure

A succinct, formal definition for a Business Procedure would say that it is a means of defining the method by which a Business Process is implemented using the current, valid, appropriate Business Mechanisms and technology. But what exactly does this mean?

Suppose that an enterprise has defined a Business Process for receiving and validating customer orders, which defines:

- What it is that starts or 'Triggers' the Business Process.
- What the Business Process is meant to achieve; this is called the Preferred Outcome.
- Where it can validly stop if the Preferred Outcome cannot be reached.
- The sequence in which the Business Process Steps should be executed in order to achieve the Preferred Outcome as effectively as possible.

Now, customer orders can be received in several different ways, for example, by telephone, email, mail, fax, etc. This means that the way in which they are most effectively processed depends on the form in which they are received. For example, an order that is received by telephone will need to be handled very differently from one that is received by email.

This is where a Business Procedure needs to be modeled, so that any variations that are dictated by the form in which the order is received can be effectively catered for.

This book is all about knowing when and how to model Business Procedures, also how to tune and optimize them so that they always deliver real business benefits.

2.5. Elements of a Business Procedure

Every valid Business Procedure must contain the following mandatory elements:

Trigger	This is a Business Event that causes the Business Procedure to start or be 'triggered.'
Preferred Outcome	This is the outcome that the enterprise would which to achieve in response to the event that triggered the Business Procedure. Every Business Procedure must have a single Preferred Outcome.
Non-Preferred Outcome	This is an outcome that the enterprise would wish to achieve when the Preferred Outcome cannot be achieved. It is a valid, if non-preferred, point at which to terminate a Business Procedure. Every Business Procedure must have at least one Non-Preferred Outcome.
Business Procedure Steps	These are the actions that, when followed in a defined sequence, bring about the Preferred Outcome for the Business Procedure or, if that cannot be attained, the Non-Preferred Outcome.

3. Preparing to Build a Business Procedure Model

Prior to building any Business Procedure Model, there are just two things that need to be in place:

- A properly modeled Business Process for the business area in question.
- A clear idea of what it is (over and above what the existing Business Process already shows us) that the Business Procedure is required to demonstrate.

NOTE: If the existing Business Process is not complete, then Procedure Modeling ought not be used as a means of completing it. The Business Process Model must first be completed and then model the Business Procedure. This approach is vital in order to avoid building flawed logical structures into the Business Procedure.

Remember, Business Procedures ought only be modeled when the different paths that different Business Mechanisms take through a Business Process need to be known and made visible.

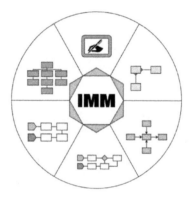

4. Business Procedure Modeling Workshop

4.1. Identifying Attendees

The attendees at the Business Procedure Modeling workshop will be business experts who:

- Have been identified by the project sponsor as experts in the business area in question.
- Are empowered to act on behalf of the business area in question.
- Can view and define the business in terms of **what** ought to be done and **how** it ought to be done.
- Do not only see the business in terms of existing organization structure, who currently does what or the existing computer systems.

4.2. Inviting Attendees

At a suitable period prior to the workshop all of the identified attendees should have been:

- Informed that they had been nominated as business experts in the area of the enterprise being modeled.
- Informed the purpose and format of the workshop.
- Informed of any materials that they should bring along.
- Supplied with a copy of the up-to-date Business Process Models for the business area in question.

If no up-to-date Business Process Models exist, then these need to be created and validated before any Business Procedure Modeling workshops are run. It is not possible to effectively model Business Procedures before Business Processes.

4.3. Approach

Each attendee should be briefed by reminding them of the purpose of the workshop and confirming that they have sufficient knowledge of the enterprise being modeled and, that they have the authority to act on behalf of their department, either by virtue of their position in the organization or because they have been nominated for the role.

Each interviewee is given a diagram of the Business Process for which the Business Procedure Model is going to be built, together with a list of the Business Mechanisms by which the Business Process can be triggered.

It is explained that the approach to modeling will be to move through the Business Process from Trigger to Outcome and model a separate path for each Business Mechanism. When each of these has been modeled, they will be merged, rationalized, tuned, and optimized.

4.4. Workshop Environment

The ideal setting is a room with a whiteboard big enough to accommodate one or two analysts and (at most) two interviewees. If possible, an electronic whiteboard from which printouts can be taken should be used.

If such a whiteboard is not available, then a reasonable quality digital camera can be used to take shots of the whiteboard. These can then be turned into proper diagrams using an appropriate CASE or diagramming tool.

After a shot of the whiteboard has been taken its clarity should be checked before the whiteboard has been wiped clean. The image should be clear and all information legible. However, until the quality is checked, **the whiteboard should not be wiped!**

5.   Building a Business Procedure Model

In the following Sections all of the stages required to build a Business Procedure Model will be worked through step-by-step from scratch based on an already modeled Business Process for receiving and validating customer orders.

Each step imagines that a modeling workshop is being run by a business analyst and attended by two suitably experienced and empowered members of the enterprise. The attendees are asked questions about all of the various means and Business Mechanisms by which customer orders can be received and validated and then a Business Procedure Model built based on their responses.

During this workshop, the analyst will:

- Validate that the Business Process on which the workshop is to be based (this is called the Focal Business Process) is correctly modeled and, if not, correct it.
- Identify all the different means by which a customer order can be received.
- Establish if each means or business mechanism requires a different route through the Business Procedure and, if so, model it.
- After building a Business Procedure for each separate business mechanism, analyze each of these, looking for similarities and differences.
- Merge the separate Business Procedures, removing all duplication.
- Tune and optimize the merged Business Procedures.

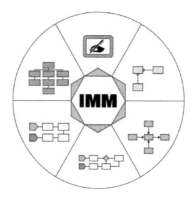

6.   Validating the Business Process

In real life a Business Procedure Modeling workshop would only be run when a Business Process has been identified that is triggered or executed by business mechanisms that need to be managed in different ways.

Before the modeling of a Business Procedure starts, a quick quality check should be carried out on the Focal Business Process in order to ensure that it contains all of the mandatory elements of a Business Process, which are:

- At least one Trigger.

- At least one Preferred Outcome.

- At least one Non-Preferred Outcome.

- A set of steps to take the Business Process from the Trigger to the Outcome(s). Each Step in a Business Process should be an Elementary Business Function (see the Glossary for a definition).

- A defined sequence in which the Steps ought to be executed.

Once all of these elements are confirmed to be in place, then modeling of the Business Procedure for this Business Process can begin building. This approach avoids taking a flawed Business Process into a modeling workshop.

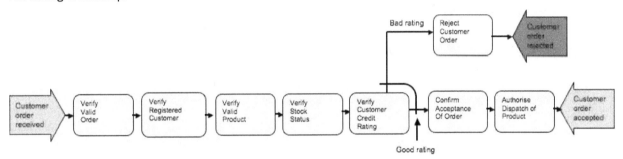

Focal Business Process for Business Procedure Modeling Workshop

The analyst presents the Focal Business Process to the workshop attendees and, talking them through it, asks them to confirm that it is correct.

Although the Focal Business Process does have all of the essential elements of a Business Process, it actually contains several shortcomings that prevent it from being considered a completely efficient Business Process. In real life the analyst would remodel this Business Process with appropriate enterprise experts in order to bring it to the appropriate quality before proceeding with the Business Procedure modeling.

However, for the purposes of modeling here, these shortcomings will prove very useful to highlight the approach to be taken when anomalies are identified during a Business Procedure Modeling workshop.

NOTE: For your convenience we have included a landscape version of the above diagram at the end of this subsection.

Landscape Diagrams from Section 6 Focal Business Process for Business Procedure Modeling Workshop

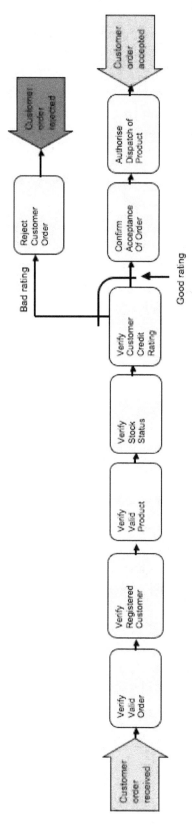

Focal Business Process for Business Procedure Modeling Workshop

6.1. Identifying Business Mechanisms

Once the analyst is happy that the Focal Business Process has been properly modeled, modeling of the Business Procedure(s) that will implement it can begin.

The first step in this is to identify all the ways in which the Focal Business Process might be triggered.

From the diagram of the Focal Business Process shown previously it can be seen that the Trigger "Customer order received" initiates the Business Process. So, the analyst asks the attendees, "In how many ways can a customer order be received?"

Imagine that they give the following list, "email, telephone, website, fax and letter." This means that for one Business Process Trigger there will be five Business Procedure Triggers.

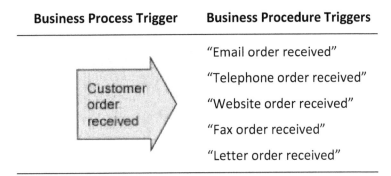

The IMM standard for writing the names of Triggers is all lower case (except the initial letter) with a verb in the **past participle,** (e.g., received) at the end.

A separate Business Procedure for each of the above Business Procedure Triggers needs to be modeled that will take the enterprise to the Preferred Business Outcome for our Focal Business Process, which is, "Customer order accepted."

NOTE: "The triggers 'fax order received' and 'letter order received' may appear outdated, and indeed, they are. However, their inclusion serves two crucial purposes. Firstly, in certain enterprises, legacy systems, contractual obligations, or legislative mandates may necessitate the exchange of information in various formats, spanning both archaic and modern methods. Their inclusion in this context illustrates the adaptability of Business Procedure Modeling, showcasing its effectiveness in modeling diverse triggering business mechanisms."

6.2. Trigger: "Email order received"

The analyst starts by modeling that part of the Business Procedure that is triggered by the event "Email order received" by asking interviewees,

> *'The Business Process Diagram for the Focal Business Process shows that the first Step to be triggered is "Verify Valid Order." Is this what happens when you receive an email order and, if so, how do you verify that it is a valid order?'*

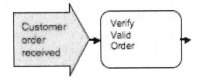

Trigger to Process Step 1

It is vital at each stage of modeling to ensure that the Business Procedure being built is fully aligned with the Focal Business Process.

Imagine that they answer the question as follows:

> *The first step is always to verify that the email is a valid order and, if not, to redirect the email, as appropriate.*

> *All sales e-mails automatically go into the "New Sales" inbox. The Sales Support Operators (we call them SSOs) all have access to this e-mail account. In between taking phone calls, they each go to the New Sales inbox and look at the e-mail at the top of the list. The Inbox is sorted by date and time so that the earliest e-mail to arrive is always at the top and the latest at the bottom.*

> *They open the e-mail and verify that it is actually ordering a product. If it is not and is some other sort or query, then it is 'Rejected.' This is done by forwarding it to the Enquiry Support Team (EST), who will automatically email customer telling them that EST is now dealing with their query and will contact them shortly. The email is then archived in the "Non-Sales" email archive folder."*

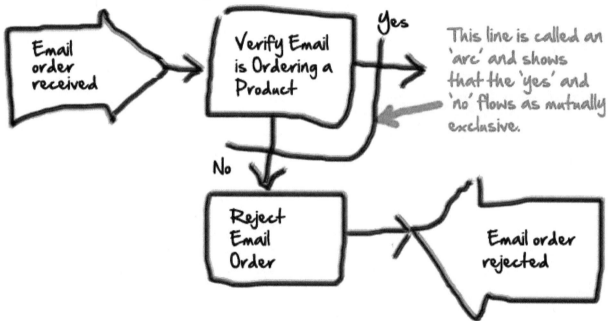

Modeling what is being said in the form of a diagram on a whiteboard is essential to enable everyone to visualize the Business Procedure. Recording what is being said is also a very powerful aid to accuracy, integrity & productivity.

It is also very important to capture all the detail associated with each Step. For example, the detail regarding the step "Reject Email Order" and how this is achieved by redirecting the email to the Enquiry Support Team, etc.

Anomalies

As can be seen from the Business Procedure diagram created above, the Business Procedure is doing something different to the Focal Business Process, in that the first step can branch and stop the Business Procedure.

The Focal Business Process diagram does not show this branching. The analyst needs to establish if this means that the Focal Business Process is wrong or that the new Business Procedure is wrong. At this point it is not clear which.

What the diagrams show is that there is an anomaly that needs to be resolved. The analyst can do several things at this point:

Raise the anomaly with the interviewees and check with them that their version in the Business Procedure is indeed correct.

If the interviewees confirm that it is, then the analyst makes a detailed note of what the anomaly is, adds the information to the diagram of the Focal Business Process so that it can later be fed back to the authors of the Focal Business Process, and then continues with the workshop.

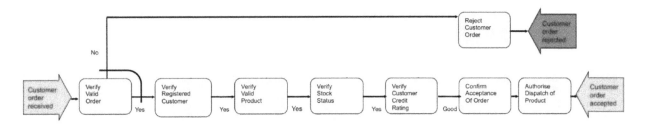

The Focal Business Process with the new detail added.

It is vital always to update the Focal Business Process. Remember that a Business Procedure is merely a means of implementing a Business Process. This always makes the Business Process the 'Master.'

NOTE: For your convenience we have included a landscape version of the above diagram at the end of this subsection.

The Next Steps

The next Business Function shown on the Business Procedure Diagram is, "Verify Customer Status." The analyst asks, "How do you do this for email orders?"

> *If the email is ordering a product, then the SSO logs into the Customer Order System (COS) and goes to the Customer Query Screen (CQ01) to verify that the writer is a registered customer.*

> *If the email is not from a registered customer the SSO rejects the request for a product, as only pre-registered customers can place orders. This is done by auto-generating an e-mail that tells the person applying the reason for rejection and advises them to contact Enquiry Support Team (EST). The original email is filed in the "Non-Customer" email archive.*

The analyst records this information and adds the tasks to the Business Procedure diagram.

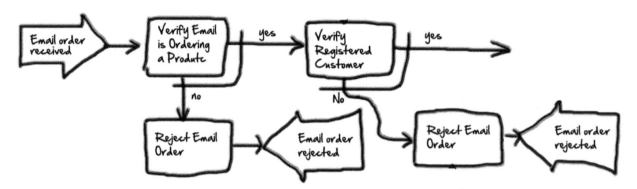

Again, it can be seen that the interviewees have introduced another branch to the Business Procedure that was not shown in the Business Process. So, the analyst again checks with the interviewees that their version is indeed correct and, if they confirm that it is, as before, then the analyst:

- Adds this branch to the Focal Business Process diagram.
- Makes a detailed note of what the anomaly is for later feedback to the authors of the Business Process.
- Continues with the workshop.

Do not worry when this happens. It is part of the modeling process.

Once again, the analyst updates the Focal Business Process diagram as shown below.

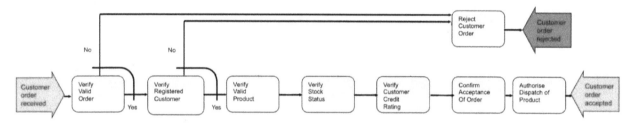

The Focal Process with the additional detail added.

NOTE: For your convenience we have included a landscape version of the above diagram at the end of this subsection.

The analyst repeats this action of updating the Focal Business Process each time that any missing detail is uncovered, such as branching, etc., that is missing from it. The analyst must then, as soon as possible, validate all of these updates with the original authors of the Focal Business Process.

The next piece of the Business Procedure the interviewees give is:

> *If the email writer is a Registered Customer, then the SSO checks to see if the Product that they have requested is a valid product. They do this by accessing the Product Catalogue Screen (PC01) in the COS.*

> *If it is not a valid product then the SSO rejects the order and informs the Customer of this by an email auto-generated by COS. The original e-mail is moved to the "Invalid Product" email archive.*

Again, there is another variation from the Focal Business Process diagram. With so many variations it does suggest that the Focal Business Process was not modeled correctly as it omitted so many ways in which the Business Process could be terminated at a Non-Preferred Outcome.

Again, the analyst makes a note of the anomaly and moves on.

As the workshop moves through each step in building this Business Procedure for handling email orders the actions taken are:

- Record what the interviewees say and add a step to the emerging Business Procedure diagram.

- Reconcile what they say with what is shown on the Focal Business Process diagram.

- If there is any inconsistency between the Business Process and the Business Procedure, then raise this anomaly with the interviewees.

- If their version is wrong, then ask them to correct it and add their amended version to the Business Procedure.

- If their version is correct, then amend the Focal Business Process diagram to reflect their version.

- Make a clear record of the detail of each Business Procedure Step as supplied by the interviewees. This detail will be vitally important later when it comes to producing Work Instructions – See the Section 18 on Work Instructions.

The analyst continues to work through the remaining steps of the Focal Business Process using the approach as detailed above.

Here is the detail that the interviewees gave for the remaining steps.

Step: Verify Product in Stock

If the product is valid, then the SSO checks to see if it is in stock in the quantity requested. If it is the SSO allocates the stock to the Customer. If it is not in stock, we inform the Customer of this and tell them that we cannot supply them with the product. We move the email to the "No Stock" archive and stop the Business Procedure.

Step: Check Customer Credit Rating

If the product is in stock, then the SSO checks the Customer's credit rating in COS. If it is flagged as 'Red' or bad, then the order is rejected and an email auto-generated by COS explaining the reason for the rejection and asking them to clear their arrears and resubmit their order when they have. The rejection of an order is flagged in COS on the Order Status Screen (OS03). The original email is moved to the "Order Rejected" email archive.

Step: Confirm Acceptance of Order

If the Customer has a good credit rating, then the SSO issues an email 'Confirmation of Order' through COS that informs the customer of the quantity to be dispatched and the anticipated dispatch date. This email and the conditions on it form the basis of the contract with the Customer.

When this email has been sent, the SSO authorizes dispatch in the Product Allocation Screen (PA01) in COS. That is where the Business Procedure for handling an email order ends.

Consolidation

The complete Business Procedure for the first Trigger Business Mechanism, namely "Email order received" has now been modeled and is shown below.

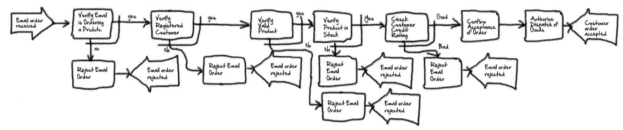

Complete Business Procedure diagram for Trigger "Email order received."

NOTE: For your convenience we have included a landscape version of the above diagram at the end of this subsection.

The next stage is to rationalize the diagram. Inspection of the whole Business Procedure shows that there are many branches that reject the email order and stop the Business Procedure. Are these all the same? Are they merely duplication? Can any of them be removed?

Never assume anything is either the same or different, always ask the question.

Looking at the diagram it shows that each time the Business Procedure branches it goes to the step "Reject Email Order" and then ends with the Non-Preferred Outcome "Email order rejected."

The analyst asked the interviewees the question, "Each time you reject an email order are the actions you take and the information you create identical?" This was their reply:

> *In general, the step "Reject Email Order" always consists of the following:*
>
> - *Define the reason for rejection and email the customer with this reason.*
> - *File the original email in the email archive linked to the check that failed and caused rejection.*
>
> *So, yes, in essence, "Reject Email Order" is always the same activity.*

This means that the Business Procedure diagram can be simplified, without losing any essential detail, to the structure shown in the diagram below.

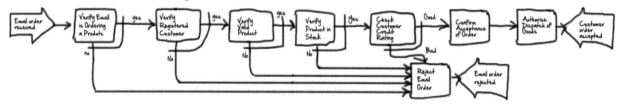

Rationalized Business Procedure Diagram for the Trigger "Email order Received."

NOTE: For your convenience we have included a landscape version of the above diagram at the end of this subsection.

Landscape Diagrams from Section 6.2 Trigger: Email Order Received

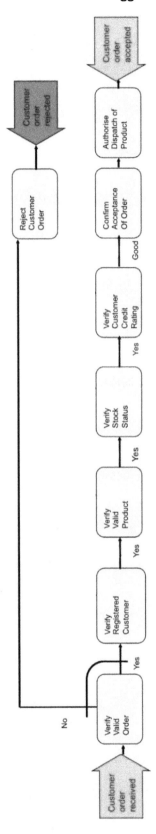

The Focal Business Process with the new detail added.

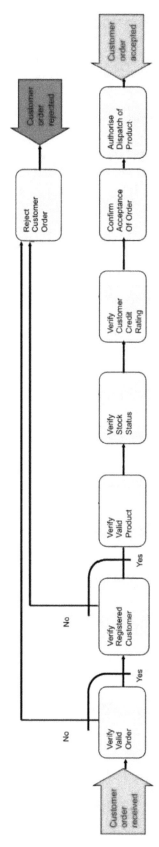

The Focal Business Process with the additional detail added.

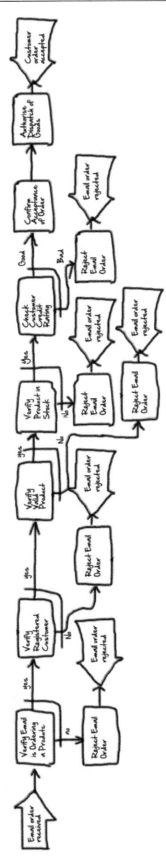

Complete Business Procedure diagram for Trigger "Email order received."

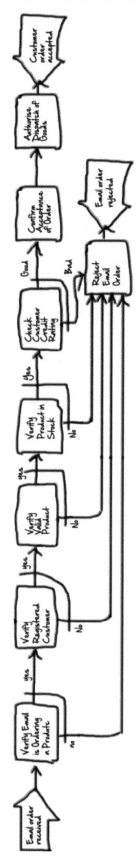

Rationalized Business Procedure Diagram for the Trigger "Email order Received."

6.3. Trigger: "telephone order received"

The second Trigger Business Mechanism is "telephone order received." The same approach is taken to modeling this as was taken with the email order. The interviewees are again reminded that the Focal Business Process Diagram shows that the first Business Function to be triggered in the Business Procedure is 'Verify Valid Order" and are asked, "Is this what happens when a telephone order is received and, if so, how is it verified that the telephone call is a valid order?'

Imagine that this is the interviewee response:

> *When the SSO answers a call, they must immediately establish that the call is placing an order and, if it is not, either end the call or redirect the call to an appropriate department.*

So when would they end the call as opposed to re-directing it?

> *If it was a definite wrong number. About 3% of all of our calls are wrong numbers. We need to politely end these as soon as possible.*

And when would you re-direct the call?

> *When the call is not placing an order but is a valid enterprise call, for example, a query on a bill payment or a delivery date. If it is for a bill payment we redirect the call to Customer Accounts, if it is regarding a delivery, we redirect it to Dispatch.*

Are these the only two department to which you would redirect calls?

> *They are the most frequent calls that we get. The SSOs can get calls that might need to be redirected to other departments. Anything that is not for Accounts or Dispatch are redirected to the Enquiry Support Team (EST) as they are best equipped to decide how to best route the call.*

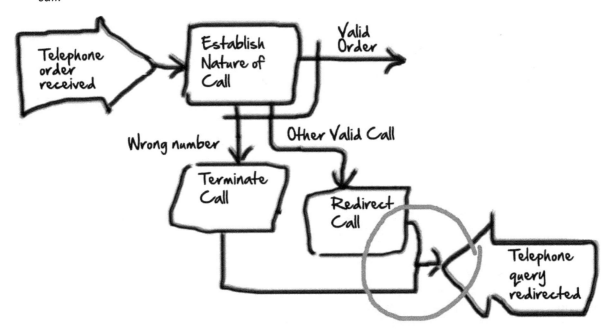

Initial part of Business Procedure with merged flow error.

The diagram above shows how the call is received, handled, and terminated. However, it does contain a crucial modeling error that the analyst made when drawing this diagram. The merged arrows in the red circle highlight this error. This structure indicates that the Non-Preferred Outcome 'Telephone query redirected' can only be reached when **both** the Business Procedure Steps of "Terminate Call" and "Redirect Call" have been completed. This situation will never arise as either the call is terminated, or it is redirected, never both.

The formal modeling conventions to be followed when modeling both Business Processes and Business Procedures are described in detail in the Section on Business Process and Procedure Modeling Conventions. (Section 9.1)

So, let us look at how this error can be removed. There are two possible solutions, as shown in the diagrams below.

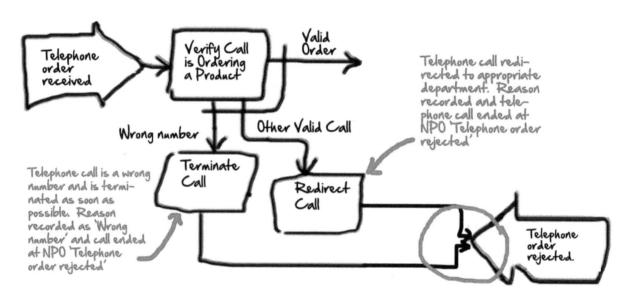

First possible solution to resolving merged flow error.

The diagram above shows the first option. The two Business Procedure Steps 'Terminate Call' and 'Redirect Call' are the same. However, the arrows emerging from these Steps do not merge, but arrive separately at the Non-Preferred Outcome 'Telephone order rejected.' This means that either one Business Procedure Step or the other will terminate the Business Procedure. The text in red expands on what happens in the Business Procedure Steps.

NOTE: For your convenience we have included a landscape version of the above diagram at the end of this subsection.

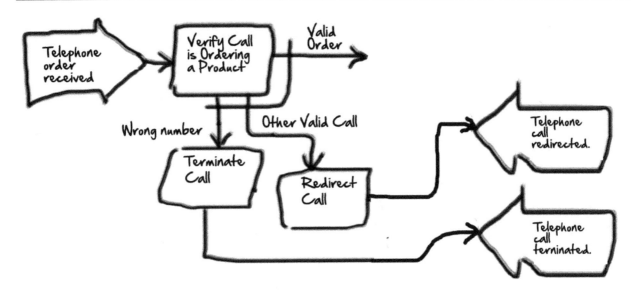

Second possible solution to resolving merged flow error.

In the second option, shown in this diagram, the Business Procedure is terminated at two separate Non-Preferred Outcomes, 'Telephone call redirected' and 'Telephone call terminated.' The major downside to this approach is that it can lead to a proliferation of Non-Preferred Outcomes, which add clutter to the diagram, without adding any real value.

The most appropriate approach to termination of Business Procedures is to terminate it at a generic Non-Preferred Outcome, such as 'Customer Order Rejected' in our example and record the reason for termination in the Business Procedure Step that does it. This ends the Business Procedure in a clear and consistent manner, while also providing a means of analyzing all reasons for termination if required at any future date.

NOTE: For your convenience we have included a landscape version of the above diagram at the end of this subsection.

By continuing to question the interviewees the analyst finds out that the rest of the Business Procedure for handling telephone orders is the same as that for handling email orders. Adding these same steps to the telephone order diagram gives the following completed diagram.

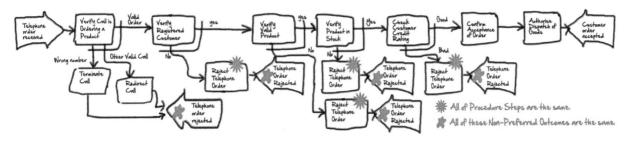

Unrationalized Business Procedure for handling telephone orders

NOTE: For your convenience we have included a landscape version of the above diagram at the end of this subsection.

As can be seen from the diagram above, there are four Business Procedure Steps and five Non-Preferred Outcomes that are repeated across the diagram.

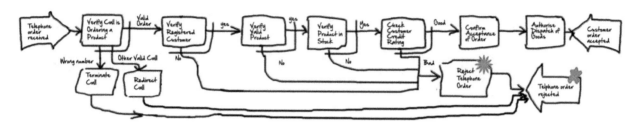

Rationalized Business Procedure for handling telephone orders

These duplicated elements are rationalized by replacing them with a single Business Procedure Step and a single Non-Preferred Outcome as shown in the diagram above.

NOTE: For your convenience we have included a landscape version of the above diagram at the end of this subsection.

Landscape Diagrams from Section 6.3 Trigger: Telephone Order Received

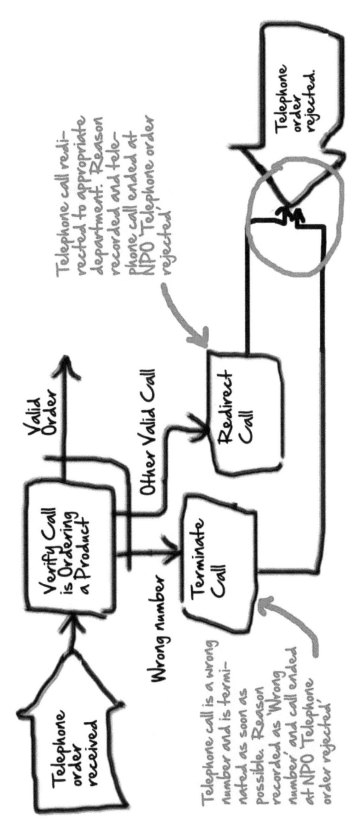

First possible solution to resolving merged flow error.

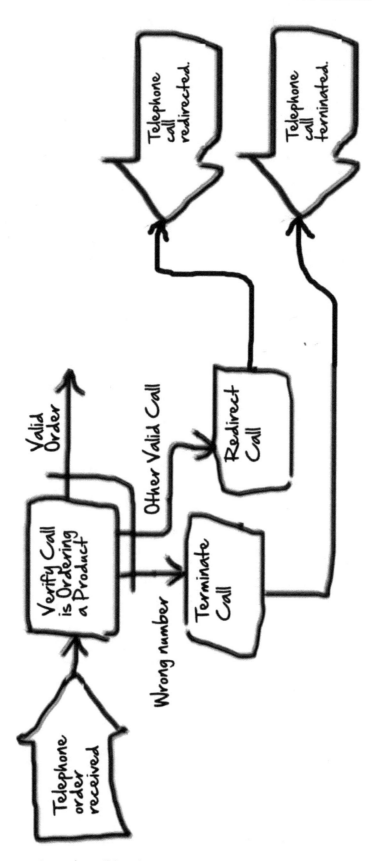

Second possible solution to resolving merged flow error.

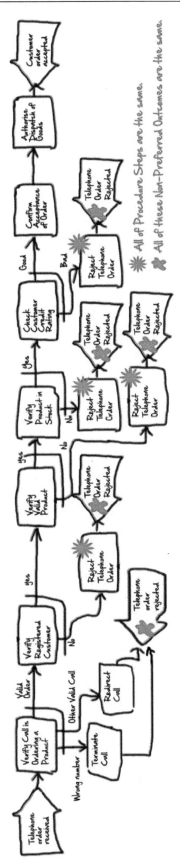

Unrationalized Business Procedure for handling telephone orders

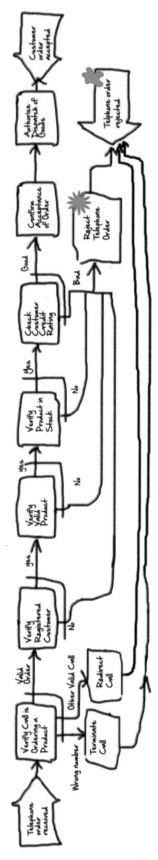

Rationalized Business Procedure for handling telephone orders

6.4. Trigger: "website order received"

Repeating the approach for the Business Mechanism "Website order received" gets the following input responses from the interviewees:

In order to check website orders the SSO logs in to the New Order Screen (WSOS01) where they will see a list of all of the submitted orders awaiting confirmation.

The website order is the simplest order of all because all of the validation has already been done on the website:

- *The order will always be a valid order as, unless a product is selected from the website, the order cannot be submitted.*

- *The customer must be a registered Customer before they can use the website and they cannot submit an order if they have a bad credit rating.*

So, all that we need to do is confirm that the order has been received and accepted.

By pressing the 'Accept' button we a) automatically get the website to send an e-mail to the customer to confirm acceptance and b) authorize dispatch of goods.

Very soon we will not even need to do this as a confirmation will be issued when the Customer submits the order, and all submitted orders will go straight through to Dispatch.

This is modeled in diagrammatic form as shown below.

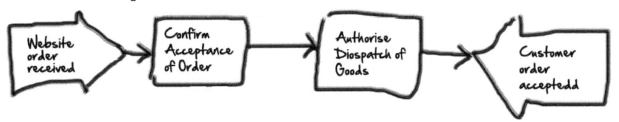

The two Business Procedure Steps that handle website orders.

6.5. Trigger: "fax order received"

The analyst now asks the interviewees about the Business Procedure for the trigger "fax order received."

All faxes arrive at the Sales Support Office fax machines, which are checked every ten minutes. When a new fax arrives, it has to be logged. This is done by entering the date, time and sender name in the Fax Logbook and the name of the person who has picked it up is entered in the 'Allocated To' column. The fax is then stamped with the time and date of receipt.

The SSO then goes through the same validation steps as they do with an email order. However, because they are now dealing with a physical piece of paper, the way that they handle it and reply or hand the query on is slightly different.

If the fax is not a valid order, then they go to the Electronic Fax Sender Screen (EFS02) in COS and issue a fax to the sending Fax number explaining that their query has been forwarded to the Enquiry Support team (EST). They stamp the original fax with "Forward to EST," together with the time and the date and put it in the "Out Tray" to be taken to the Enquiry Support Office at the next mail pickup.

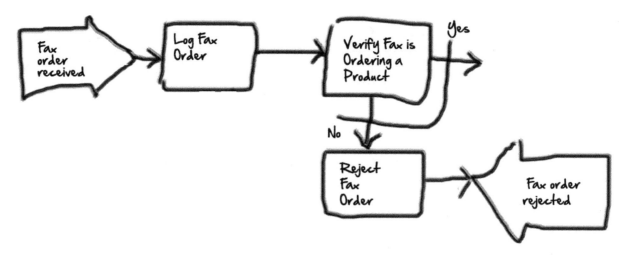

Initial Business Procedure Steps for registering a fax order.

The SSO then goes to the Customer Query Screen (CQ01) in the Customer Order System (COS) to see if the sender of the Fax is a registered customer. If they are not, they go to the Electronic Fax Sender Screen (EFS02) in COS and issue a fax to the sending Fax number explaining that we can only take orders from registered customers. This fax also explains to them how to go about registering as a customer.

If the sender is a Registered Customer, then the SSO checks to see if the Product that they have requested is a valid product. They do this by accessing the Product Catalogue Screen (PC01) in the COS. If it is not a valid product then the SSO rejects the order and informs the Customer of this by an auto-generated Fax through Screen EFS02. The original Fax is stamped "Invalid Product" and put into the "To Be Filed" tray.

If the product is in stock, then the SSO checks the Customer's credit rating in COS. If it is flagged as 'Red' or bad, then the order is rejected and a Fax auto-generated by COS explaining the reason for the rejection and asking them to clear their arrears and resubmit their order when they have. The rejection of an order is flagged in COS on the Order Status Screen (OS03). The original Fax is "Rejected Bad Credit," together with the data and time and put in the "To Be Filed" tray.

If the Customer has a good credit rating, then the SSO authorizes dispatch in the Product Allocation Screen (PA01) in COS. They also issue a fax Confirmation of Order through Screen EFS02 in COS that informs the customer of the quantity to be dispatched and the anticipated dispatch date. This forms the basis of the contract with the Customer.

They then stamp the Fax as "Dispatch Authorized," together with the time and date and place it in the "To Be Filed" tray.

This ends the Business Procedure for a fax order.

The diagram for this Business Procedure will be exactly the same as that for the email order, except that for the very first step of registering the fax.

6.6.   Trigger: "letter order received"

For the final order, the analyst asks the interviewees, "What happens when a letter arrives?"

That is exactly the same as for the fax order except at each stage they actually produce a letter instead of a fax when they want to correspond with the customer. Once again, because the diagram would be exactly the same, we will not show it here at the moment.

6.7.   Merging The Business Procedures

From the model built based on the interviewee responses, it is clear that all the Business Procedures are identical from the step "Verify Registered Customer" onwards, with the exception of that for the website order. So, all of those steps can be merged immediately.

All that is left to do is consolidate and merge, where possible, all of the initial steps. These have all been brought together here.

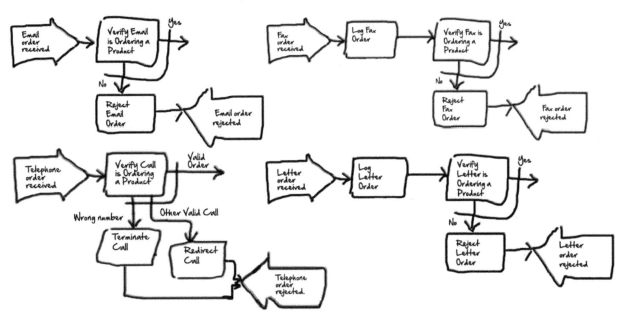

The four separate front-end Business Procedure Models

From the above diagram it can see that the steps for letter and fax have an identical shape. This suggests that they might be the same thing. Indeed, they are and can be easily merged simply by using the term "letter or fax" in the text.

NOTE: For your convenience we have included a landscape version of the above diagram at the end of this subsection.

Further inspection shows that the first step in the email order Business Procedure is the same as the second step in the fax/letter Business Procedure. This means that they can be merged at the second step.

Making both of these amendments will gives the following diagram.

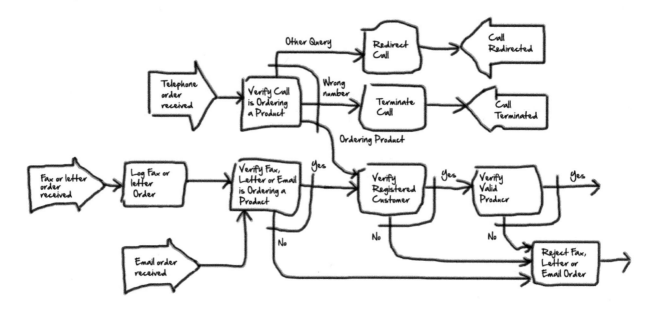

The four separate front-end Business Procedures are merged into one.

NOTE: For your convenience we have included a landscape version of the above diagram at the end of this subsection.

All that is now left is the trigger "Website order received." This skips all of the steps of the other Business Procedures right up to "Confirm Acceptance of Order." So, to merge this Business Procedure with Business Procedures for all of the other triggers, all that is needed is to show the trigger "Website order received" triggering the step "Confirm Acceptance of Order."

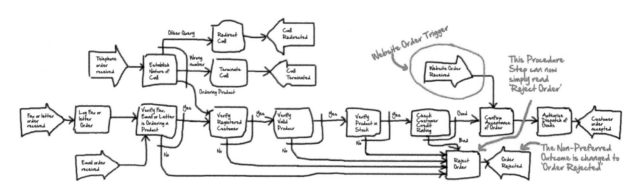

Combined Business Procedure diagram for all triggers

NOTE: For your convenience we have included a landscape version of the above diagram at the end of this subsection.

Landscape Diagrams from Section 6.7 Merging the Business Procedures.

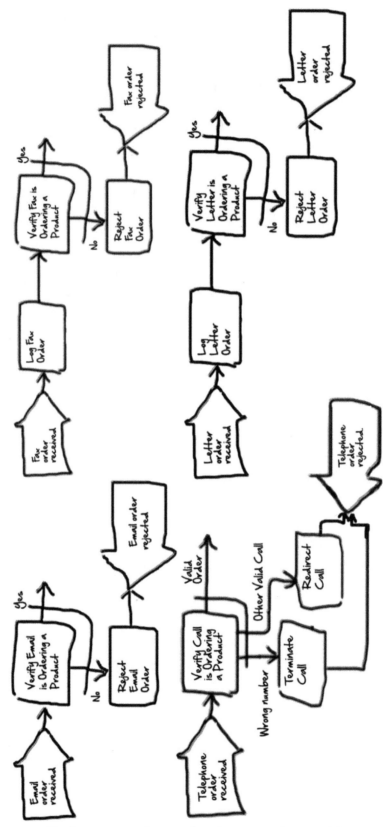

The four separate front-end Business Procedure Models

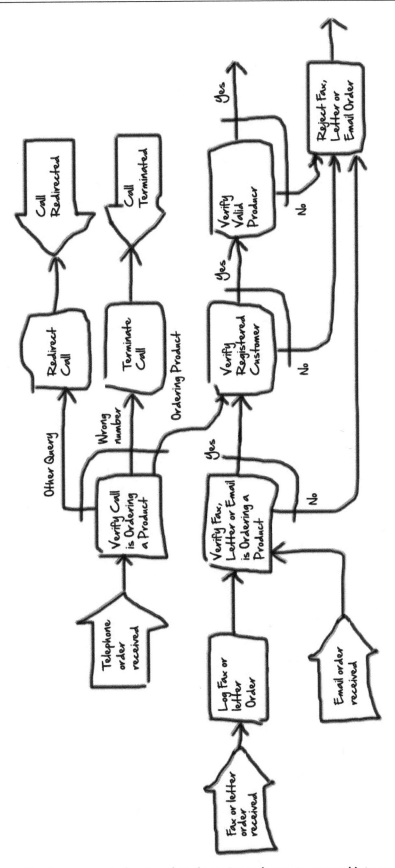

The four separate front-end Business Procedures are merged into one.

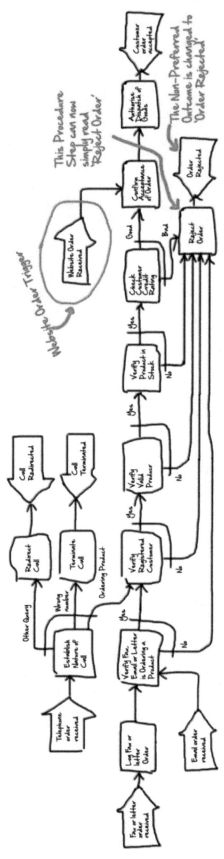

Combined Business Procedure diagram for all triggers

7. Tuning Business Procedures

It costs time and, therefore, money to carry out Business Procedures. For this reason, it is important that they are both effective and efficient. Consequently, a vital stage in building any Business Procedure is to ensure that it is 'tuned.'

The best way to ensure that a Business Procedure is tuned is to ensure that the Business Process on which it is based has already been fully tuned. This is an essential modeling rule to remember – *always tune the Business Process first!*

Business Processes should be tuned when they are being built in a modeling workshop. An untuned Business Process is an incomplete Business Process, which ought not be implemented in the enterprise. When tuning a Business Process, the analysts and interviewees work closely together in order to make the Business Process as effective and efficient as possible. The analysts bring their analysis and tuning expertise. The interviewees, who are the business experts, provide the pragmatic and detailed business knowledge that ensures that the tuning will not breach any business policies, standards, or legal requirements.

7.1. Effectiveness and Efficiency

An effective Business Process is one that is capable of achieving the Business Process Preferred Outcome time after time in a structured and consistent manner that generates maximum revenue at minimum cost.

An efficient Business Process is an effective Business Process that reaches the desired Outcome in the fewest possible steps. But that is only half the story. A really efficient Business Process is one that also reaches all Non-Preferred Outcomes in the fewest possible steps.

This means that, if the Business Process is going to be stopped short of the Preferred Outcome, this should happen as soon as possible in the execution of the Business Process. This is counter-intuitive to many people, especially to those involved in sales, whose natural inclination is to keep the Business Process heading toward the Preferred Outcome for as long as possible in the hope that they will be able to 'close the deal.'

This is a very inefficient approach. The fact is that, if a condition exists that is going to stop the Business Process, then, like it or not, the Business Process is going to stop! It is far better to stop it sooner rather than later as each unnecessary step taken is wasted effort and cost incurs costs.

It is also a bad approach from the point of view of customer service because, if the Business Process is not going to get to the Preferred Outcome, the customer should be made aware of this as soon as possible. To do anything else would be misleading and could jeopardize customer good will.

7.2. Ranking Non-Preferred Outcomes

Making Non-Preferred Outcomes happen as soon as possible is a very powerful, structured, and repeatable technique for tuning a Business Process. The steps in this technique are:

- Identify all possible conditions in which a Business Process would be terminated at a Non-Preferred Outcome.
- Rank these conditions – least desirable first.
- Test for each condition as early as possible in the Business Process.
- If the condition applies, test to see if there is an alternative option.

- If there is no alternative, then stop the Business Process at that point.
- Have a Non-Preferred Outcome at which to stop the Business Process.

7.3. Tuning Example

Let us look at the Focal Business Process for accepting customer orders that we have just modeled as a Business Procedure and see how we can tune it, following the approach described above. Once we have tuned the Business Process, we will then be able to quickly tune the newly modeled Business Procedure.

Firstly, we must identify and list all of the conditions under which the Business Process could be halted and result in a Non-Preferred Outcome. These are:

- The 'order' is not actually an order.
- The enterprise does not sell the product being requested.
- There is currently no stock of the required product.
- The requestor is not a Registered Customer.
- Registered Customer has a bad debt record.

We must now rank these, 'least desirable' first. There are two categories of 'least desirable':

- Category 1: The enterprise would not want to proceed.
- Category 2: The customer might not want to proceed.

We should always look for Category 1 conditions first as these are essential in minimizing risk to the enterprise.

So, we ask the question, "Are there any conditions under which the enterprise might not want to proceed with this order?" In our example there are three conditions that fall into this category:

1. The order is not actually a valid order.
2. The person placing the order is not a Registered Customer.
3. The person placing the order is a Registered Customer but has a bad credit rating.

Which of these should we check for first?

If the order is not a valid order, then there is no point in proceeding from either the enterprise or customer point of view, so this condition should be tested for first.

If the person placing the order is not a Registered Customer, then the enterprise would not want to proceed, so there would be no need to check on the credit rating. This means that the check to see if they are a registered customer should come before the check for credit rating.

This means that the ranking for our Category 1 occurrences is the 1,2, 3 order in which they were listed above.

We then look for Category 2 conditions by asking the question, "Are there any conditions under which the customer might not want to proceed with a sale?"

In our example there are also two conditions in this category:

1. The enterprise does not sell a product that would meet the customer's needs.
2. There is no stock of the required product.

Which of these conditions should we test for first?

Well, there would be little point of checking to see if we had stock of a product if the enterprise did not sell a suitable product, so we should test for the existence of a suitable product first.

So, we have now identified and ranked all conditions that could lead to our Business Process being terminated at a Non-Preferred Outcome and they are, in the order in which they should be tested for:

- Order is not a valid order.
- Requestor is not a Registered Customer.
- Registered Customer has a bad debt record.
- The enterprise does not sell a product to meet the customer's needs.
- There is currently no stock of the required product.

Let us look at the Focal Business Process and see if it:

- Has a Business Process Step that tests for all of these conditions listed above.
- Test for the conditions in the order in which they have been ranked.
- Has a Business Process Step that ends the Business Process.
- Has a Non-Preferred Outcome at which to safely terminate the Business Process.

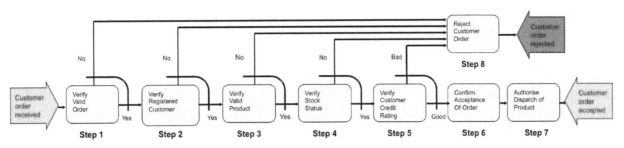

Untuned Focal Business Process diagram

The above diagram does indeed test for all the conditions listed, Steps 1 through 5. Business Process Step 8 ends the Business Process at a clearly defined Non-Preferred Outcome, "Customer order rejected".

However, the Business Process does not test for all of the terminating conditions in the order in which they were ranked, following our ranking criteria.

The test at Step 5 should be carried out *before* the test at Step 3. So let us change the sequence to make this happen.

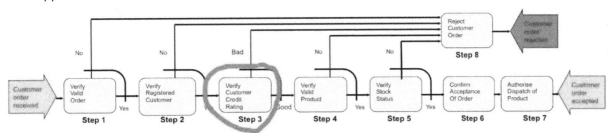

Tuned Focal Business Process diagram.

In the diagram above, all the terminating conditions are tested for in the order defined by the defined tuning ranking criteria. 'Verify Customer Credit Rating' is now Step 3 as opposed to Step 5 in the Business Process.

The Business Process is now fully tuned, as will be any Business Procedure based on the Business Process.

NOTE: For your convenience we have included a landscape version of the two diagrams above, at the end of this subsection.

Landscape Diagrams from Section 7.3 Tuning Example

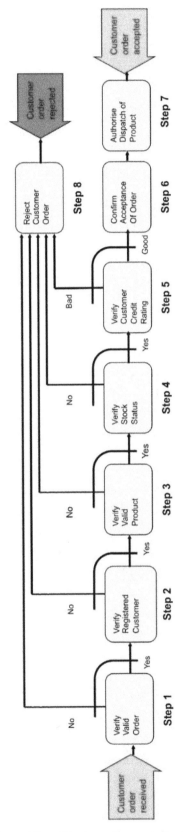

Untuned Focal Business Process diagram

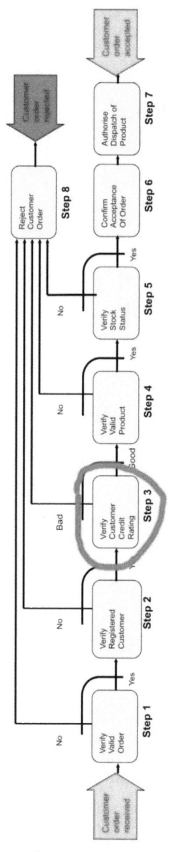

Tuned Focal Business Process diagram.

8.   Optimizing Business Processes

Although the Focal Business Process has been tuned, it has not yet been *optimized*. What do we mean by this?

When we tuned our Business Process, we achieved three main objectives:

- We minimized risk to the enterprise by terminating it if a risk existed.
- We minimized the cost of carrying out the Business Process by terminating it as soon as possible.
- We minimized any unnecessarily irritation for customers by not prolonging a Business Process that could not be completed.

What we did not do was to maximize the chances of having the Business Process proceed to the Preferred Outcome, without in any way presenting any increased risk to the enterprise.

Maximizing the chances of a successful outcome for a Business Process is called Optimizing the Business Process and is achieved quite easily. Each time that a condition exists that would call for the Business Process to be terminated, we test to see if an alternative outcome can be achieved. Let us look at our tuned Focal Business Process and see how this is done.

We will build a list of the terminating conditions and, for each one, identify a test for an alternative condition or action that would help the Business Process to proceed towards the Preferred Outcome.

Terminating Condition	Business Function to Find an Alternative Condition	Description
Invalid Order	None	There is not alternative that will move the Business Process nearer to the Preferred Outcome of 'Customer order accepted' as the contacting party does not want to purchase anything, so the Business Process should be immediately terminated.
Requestor is not a registered customer.	Submit Application for Registration	Having established that the party placing the order is not currently a registered customer, they are asked if they would like to register. If they would, then this Business Function is initiated, and an Application for Registration submitted. If the application is accepted, then the Business Process can be resumed at the next step, 'Verify Customer Credit Rating.'
Customer has bad debt record.	Request Payment of Outstanding Balance.	If the Customer currently has a bad credit rating with the enterprise, then they can be asked to pay off the outstanding balance of their account, plus a payment in advance, if appropriate, before dispatching their order. If they agree to do so, then the Business Process can continue to check that the enterprise sells the product that they are requesting.

Terminating Condition	Business Function to Find an Alternative Condition	Description
No suitable product.	Check for Alternative Product	If the enterprise does not sell the exact product that the customer is ordering, then every effort should be made to see if it sells an alternative. If one exists and the customer would be willing to purchase it, then the Business Process can continue and check to see if there is a product in stock.
No stock.	Check to see if Customer Can Wait for Stock to Arrive.	If there is no stock of the selected product then a check should be made to see if the customer can wait for stock to arrive. If they can wait, then the Business Process can continue to the next step of Confirm Acceptance of Order. If they cannot wait, then the Business Process is terminated.

Adding all these extra steps to the Business Process for handling customer orders gives us the Business Process diagram shown below.

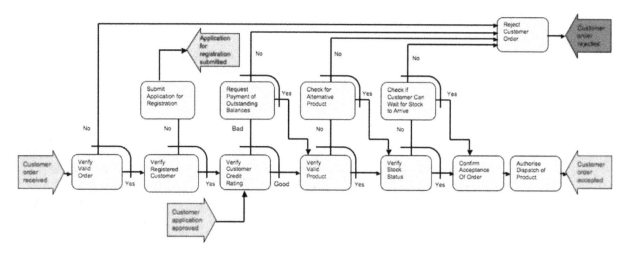

Tuned and Optimized Business Process Model for Receiving and Validating Customer Orders

NOTE: For your convenience we have included a landscape version of the above diagram at the end of this subsection.

Using this approach of looking for an action that can reverse or mitigate the terminating condition enables the Business Process to always move forward towards the Preferred Outcome.

When Business Process Steps have been added in this way that check for all possible alternative conditions, then the Business Process is both tuned and fully optimized.

The proviso is that time should not be wasted and the risk to the enterprise should not be increased.

Landscape Diagrams from Section 8 Optimizing Business Processes

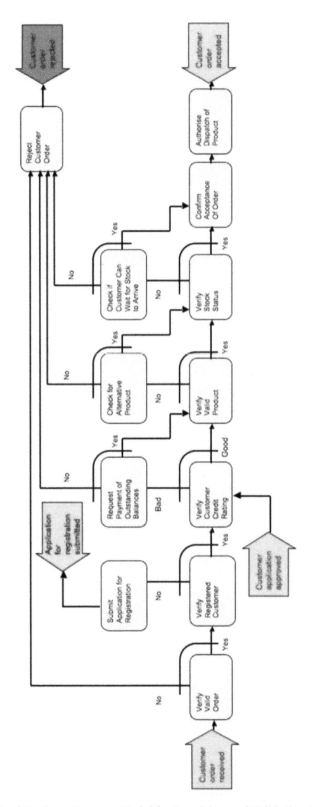

Tuned and Optimized Business Process Model for Receiving and Validating Customer Orders

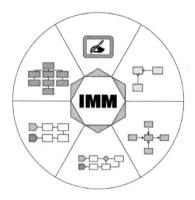

9.   Aligning Models

9.1.   Aligning Business Process and Business Procedure

Now that we have fully tuned and optimized the Business Process for accepting customer orders, we need to ensure that it is synchronized with all other related models in the enterprise.

The first model to be updated is the Business Procedure that we were building for accepting customer orders, to ensure that it fully reflects the tuning and optimization done to the Business Process.

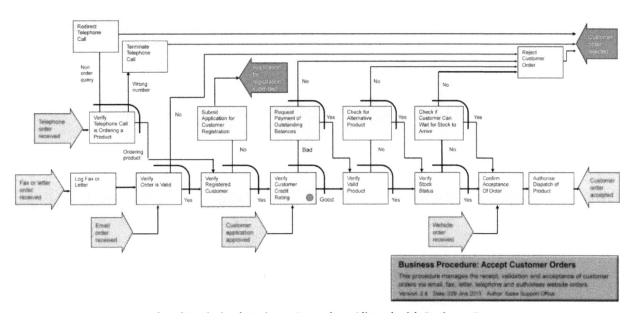

Tuned and Optimized Business Procedure Aligned with Business Process

The Business Procedure diagram above shows that 'Verify Customer Credit Rating' has been brought forward (marked with a red dot ●) and the four extra steps that look for alternatives have also been added.

The diagram shows the Business Procedure updated to fully reflect the tuning and optimization that was done in the Business Process.

NOTE: For your convenience we have included a landscape version of the above diagram at the end of this subsection.

The steps in the Business Procedure Diagram are shown as rectangles ▢ as opposed to rounded boxes ▢ as they are shown in the Business Process Diagram. This is a very useful modeling convention that enables Business Process Models and Business Procedure Models to be quickly differentiated.

Landscape Diagrams from Section 9.1 Aligning Business Process and Business Procedure

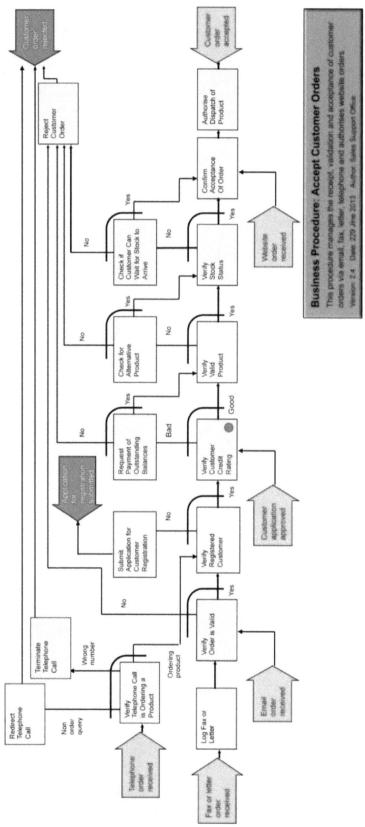

Tuned and Optimized Business Procedure Aligned with Business Process

9.2. Aligning with Business Function Model

The second model with which we need to synchronize is the Business Function Model for the enterprise. Each step that we added to the Business Process must also be added as a Business Function to the Business Function Model.

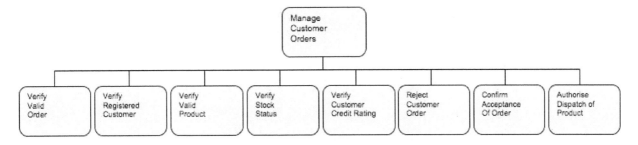

Original Business Function Model

The above diagram represents the original leg of the Business Function Model (BFM) that holds the Business Functions that deal with accepting customer orders. We now need to add the additional optimizing steps from our Business Process to this.

NOTE: For your convenience we have included a landscape version of the above diagram at the end of this subsection.

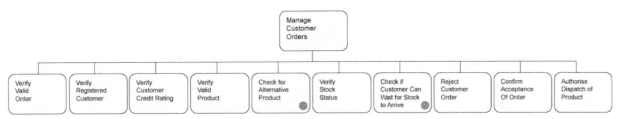

Business Function Model with Additional Business Functions Added

The above diagram shows two of the Business Functions added to this leg of the BFM namely, 'Check for Alternative Product' and 'Check if Customer Can Wait for Stock to Arrive' – each marked with a red dot.

NOTE: For your convenience we have included a landscape version of the above diagram at the end of this subsection.

This leaves two other Business Functions, 'Submit Application for Registration' and 'Request Payment of Outstanding Balance,' that have still to be added. However, although they do belong in the BFM, they do not belong on this leg.

'Submit Application for Registration' would belong on that leg of the BFM that deals with recruiting and registering new customers. 'Request Payment of Outstanding Balance' belongs on the leg that deals with revenue management, accounts receivable activities, etc.

Landscape Diagrams from Section 9.2 Aligning with Business Function Models

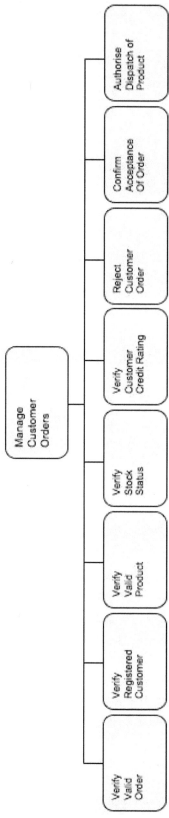

Original Business Function Model

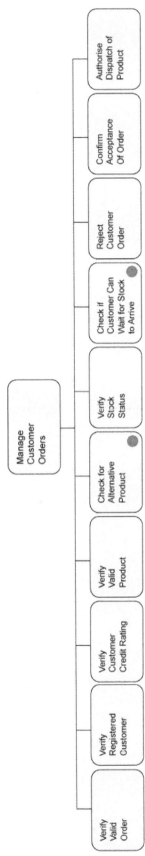

Business Function Model with Additional Business Functions Added

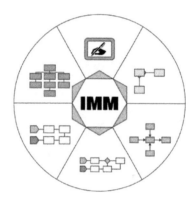

10. Adding Detail to Business Procedures

The elements in the table in the previous Section will be adequate to meet the needs of Business Procedure modeling in most business situations. However, there will be times when it is helpful to add extra information to Business Procedure models to make clear precisely what is happening.

In this section we will look at various ways of adding useful additional elements to Business Procedures in order to provide better understanding of drivers, actions, outcomes, etc.

10.1. Adding Information Flow

Providing the ability to be able to see the flow of information into and out of a Business Procedure can be very helpful in certain situations. However, this needs to be done judiciously or, rather than bringing clarity, it just adds confusion.

Information flow is shown on a Business Procedure model as a dotted line arrow into or out of a Business Procedure Step.

One area where showing the information flow is particularly helpful is when the arrival of a particular piece of information triggers the Business Procedure.

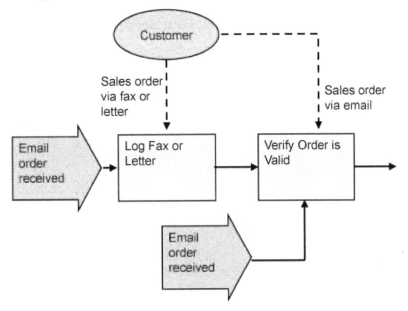

Information Flow as a Trigger

The above diagram is a segment from the Business Procedure that accepts sales orders from customers.

To clearly show that the arrival of information in a particular format is a Trigger for this Business Procedure, we display this information flow on the Business Procedure model. The information flow is shown as a dotted arrow coming from Customer into the Business Procedure Step that receives and initially deals with it.

When shown as an ellipse on a Business Procedure model in this way, Customer is termed an External Entity, which is any entity external to the enterprise with which the enterprise has, or might have, a commercial relationship.

In the Business Procedure we modeled earlier for accepting customer orders, there was a point where applications for registration were submitted for unregistered customers and the Business Procedure stopped at a Non-Preferred Outcome.

We can show more clearly what happens at this point in the Business Procedure by adding an Information Flow showing the application being passed to a Business Function (Business Process Step) in the Business Process that handles applications for customer registration.

We can also show how our Business Procedure is restarted when the application for registration is approved and the initial customer credit rating is received back from the Business Function (Business Process Step) that approves customer registrations.

Although we are modeling a Business Procedure, the information flow going out is shown going to a Business Function as opposed to a Business Procedure Step. This is the correct way of modeling this scenario as the destination is external to the Business Procedure being modeled and should therefore be modeled at the most generic level, which is Business Function.

The same is true of the information flow being received back regarding the initial customer credit rating. This also comes from a source external to the Business Procedure being modeled and should be shown at a generic level, which is a Business Function.

We will cover information flows into and out of Business Processes and Business Procedures in more detail later on when we look a Swim Lanes in section 13 and Worldview in section 14.

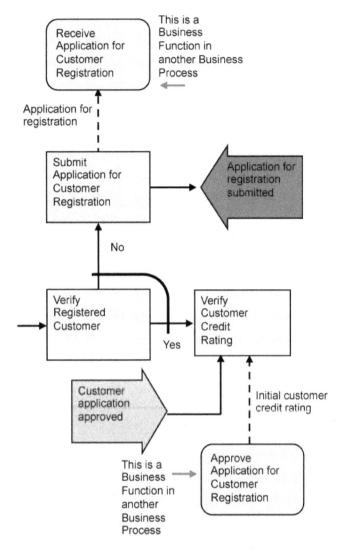

Information Flow to and from Business Functions

10.2. Adding Document Flow

Sometimes it can be useful to show the flow of physical documents into and out of specific Business Procedure steps. This is achieved in much the same way as information flows is modeled, except that, instead of using dotted arrows to show information flow, we use block arrows containing the name of the document to indicate the document flow.

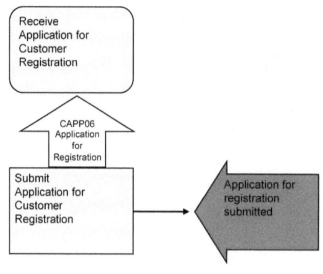

Outward Document Flow

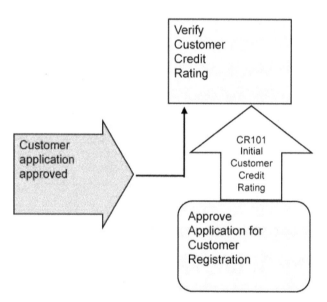

Inward Document Flow

Material and resource flow can be shown in the same way as document flow simply by labeling the block arrows with the name of the material or resource.

However, the main thing to remember here is that these flows should only be added to a Business Procedure model when they help to bring extra clarity to a specific facet of the Business Procedure.

11. Further Definitions

11.1. Workflow

The term "Workflow" should not be confused with the flow of control through a Business Process or a Business Procedure. It refers to the scheduling, managing and, monitoring the flow of **work** through a specific Business Process or Business Procedure of an enterprise to ensure that it is performed, and products and services, delivered in accordance with all relevant Service Level Agreements (SLAs), policy, objectives, or any other relevant enterprise values.

11.2. Discrete Business Process Rule

> *"Every Business Process must be capable of being defined as the execution of a discrete, coherent set of Elementary Business Functions with a **single** Preferred Outcome. If the Preferred Outcome is not attainable then a set of predefined Non-Preferred Outcomes must be attainable in a coherent, predefined manner. If a Business Process does not conform to this rule, it is not a valid Business Process."*

"Does this Business Process conform to the discrete Business Process rule?" is a vital question for analysts to ask of themselves to check that the Business Process they are modeling is effective and efficient.

11.3. 'End to End' Business Process

An 'end-to-end' Business Process is a special occurrence of a contiguous Business Process that answers special questions for business management. Such questions might be:

> "What are the activities the business must do from identifying and recruiting a new customer to supplying their first purchase, billing them, and receiving payment? How long does this take and what does it cost?"

11.4. Super Business Process

This is a term that in the past has been applied to an 'end-to-end' Business Process covering 'all business activities.' **There is no such thing as a 'Super Business Process' and it is a term to be avoided.** Attempts to model super Business Processes have had people trying to fit all Business Processes onto one diagram and have resulted, unsurprisingly, in chaos.

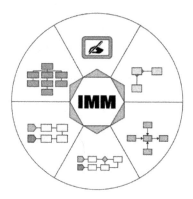

12. Contiguous Business Processes

12.1. Definition

A contiguous Business Process is a Business Process comprising two or more discrete Business Processes whose Triggers and Outcomes coincide. These Business Processes are called contiguous because they 'touch.' But they are not <u>continuous</u>.

The concept of contiguous Business Processes avoids the need for attempts to create a "Super Business Process." It allows a business to have the operational power and flexibility provided by short, discreet Business Processes, while at the same time provide an 'end-to-end' view of Business Processes when required.

All Business Processes in a business should be discrete. Not all Business Processes will be contiguous.

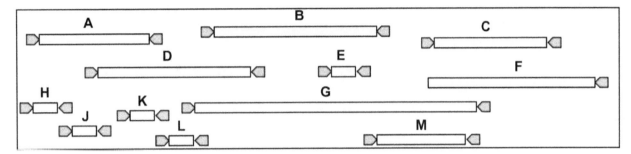

Non-Contiguous Business Processes

The diagram above represents a set of Business Processes that are completely disjointed. In a business such as this the management could never ask questions such as:

> "What Business Functions must we perform, and in what order, which will enable us to receive an order, dispatch the appropriate products and get payment, in full, from the customer? How long, on average, does this take?"

The following diagram shows how, with some rationalization, many of the Business Processes can be made contiguous. This is achieved, not by the creation of a 'super Business Process' but by simply aligning the Outcomes and Triggers of discrete Business Processes.

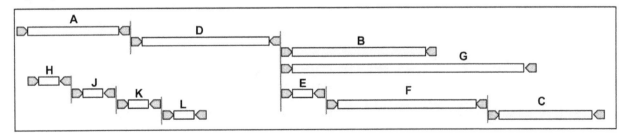

Contiguous Business Processes

The red vertical lines in this diagram represent the alignment of Outcomes and Triggers. Each Outcome represents a key Milestone in Business Process execution, which may also be the trigger for another Business Process.

Maintaining discrete Business Processes as opposed to merging Business Processes together is very important as this gives the business maximum flexibility as well as maximum control over Business Process modeling, resourcing, and execution. As can be seen from the diagram not all Business Processes need to be made contiguous.

This approach should make it clear that there is never a need to try to create a 'super Business Process' by merging all Business Processes into one!

12.2. Modeling Contiguous Business Processes

This section describes how to model Contiguous Business Processes or Business Procedures for all or part of an enterprise in a simple, yet very powerful way.

The elements on a Contiguous Business Process diagram will be:

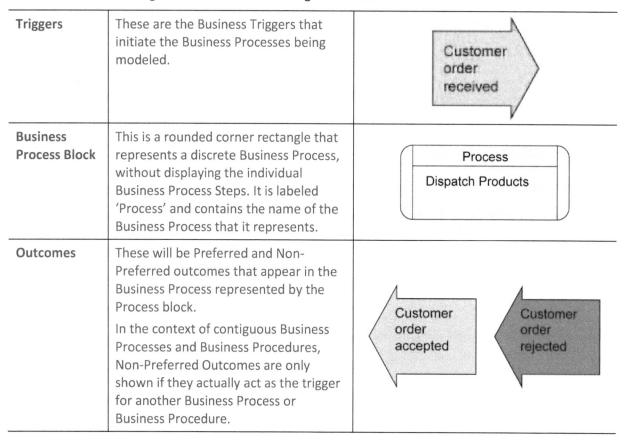

Triggers	These are the Business Triggers that initiate the Business Processes being modeled.	
Business Process Block	This is a rounded corner rectangle that represents a discrete Business Process, without displaying the individual Business Process Steps. It is labeled 'Process' and contains the name of the Business Process that it represents.	
Outcomes	These will be Preferred and Non-Preferred outcomes that appear in the Business Process represented by the Process block. In the context of contiguous Business Processes and Business Procedures, Non-Preferred Outcomes are only shown if they actually act as the trigger for another Business Process or Business Procedure.	

The steps to follow to model contiguous Business Processes:

- Build a list of all events that would result in the triggering of a Business Process inside the enterprise.
- List the Business Processes triggered by these listed events.
- List both the Preferred and Non-Preferred Outcomes for all the identified Business Processes.
- Identify all Business Processes that are triggered by events that are the Outcomes of Business Processes.
- Build a diagram showing how these Triggers, Business Processes and Outcomes are linked.

12.3. Example

The following diagram displays a simple, yet powerful example of how discrete Business Processes can be linked together to get from the triggering Event, "Customer order received" to the Preferred Outcome of "Customer bill paid."

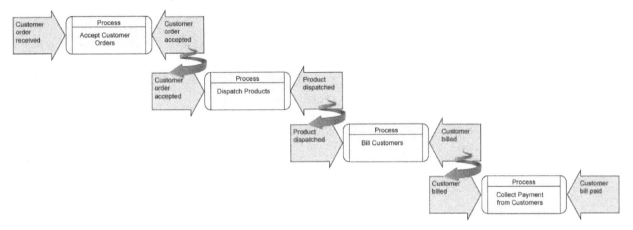

Example of Contiguous Business Processes

Each Business Process is discrete and meets its objective by arriving at its Preferred Outcome. Where the Outcome of one Business Process equates to the Trigger for another Business Process, these Outcomes and Triggers are aligned, as shown in the above diagram.

Using this technique, we can model and display the interdependency of Business Processes across the whole of an enterprise of any size.

NOTE: For your convenience we have included a landscape version of the above diagram at the end of this subsection.

Landscape Diagrams from Section 12.3 Contiguous Business Processes: Example

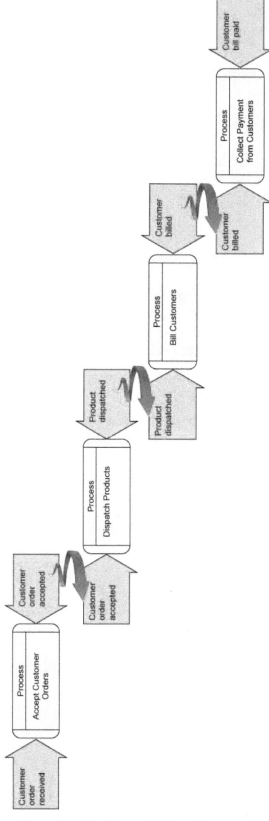

Example of Contiguous Business Processes

13. Swim Lanes

When modeling Business Procedures it is often important to know what part of the organization does each step in the Business Procedure, or the location at which each step is done, or what job role does each step.

The use of 'Swim Lanes' is an effective way to show these things. Swim Lanes are rectangles stretched across the Business Procedure diagram and are used to represent relevant:

- Business departments
- Business locations
- Job roles
- Types of technology

Each step in the Business Procedure is then placed in a Swim Lane. The term 'Swim Lane' came about by somebody thinking that the horizontal rectangles across the page looked like the lanes in a swimming pool viewed from above!!

13.1. Swim Lanes as Business Departments

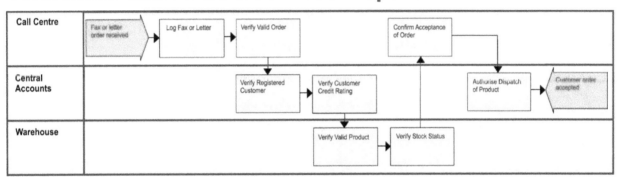

Swim lanes as business departments

The above diagram is an example of a Business Procedure model using Swim Lanes to represent Business Departments. What does this diagram tell us?

- There are three departments involved in the Business Process.
- The Business Procedure is triggered in the Call Centre and ends in Central Accounts.
- After 'Verify Valid Order' responsibility passes from the Call Centre to Central Accounts.
- After 'Verify Customer Credit Rating' responsibility passes from Central Accounts to Warehouse.
- After 'Verify Stock Status' responsibility passes from Warehouse to 'Call Centre.'
- After 'Confirm Acceptance of Order' responsibility passes from Call Centre to Central Accounts, where the Business Process ends.

NOTE: For your convenience we have included a landscape version of the above diagram at the end of this subsection.

There are major benefits in modeling Business Procedure in Swim Lanes in this way. It allows the enterprise to answer questions such as:

- How many enterprise departments are involved in the Business Process?
- Is the Business Procedure fragmented because of too many departments?
- How many times during the Business Procedure does responsibility pass from one department to another?

These 'handoffs' between departments represent potential problems in a Business Procedure because:

- With the handoff comes a change of control and responsibility.
- Different departments may have different enterprise objectives and different performance indicators that may not align with each other.
- The different departments may use different computer systems and different technologies.

Landscape Diagram from Section 13.1 Swim Lanes as Business Departments

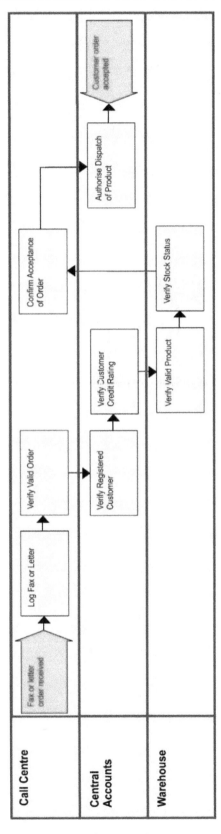

Swim lanes as business departments

13.2. Swim Lanes as Locations

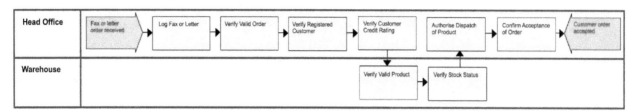

Swim lanes as business locations

In the above diagram the Swim Lanes represent the Locations at which the Business Procedure is carried out. The diagram tells us:

- The Business Procedure is carried out at two locations, Head Office, and Warehouse.
- That there needs to be effective communication and technology links between these two Locations to be able to complete customer orders.

This may all seem self-evident from such a simple diagram but in a real-life situation the Business Procedure could be much larger and more detailed and there could be numerous Locations involved. In such circumstances the Swim Lane representation of a Business Procedure can enable problems and solutions to be visualized that might not be possible to appreciate using text or matrices (see Section 13.4 Swim Lanes vs Matrices).

NOTE: For your convenience we have included a landscape version of the above diagram at the end of this subsection.

Landscape Diagram from Section 13.2 Swim Lanes as Locations

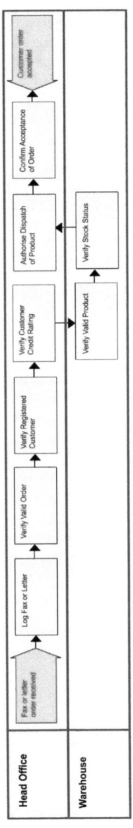

Swim Lanes as Locations

13.3. Swim Lanes as Job Roles

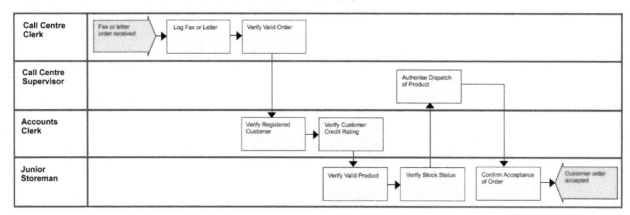

Swim lanes as Job Roles

The above diagram shows Swim Lanes being used to represent job roles.

This diagram tells the enterprise:

- There are four Job Roles involved with this Procedure.
- There are four handoffs involved during the execution of the Business Procedure.
- The Business Procedure Steps in which each of these job roles will require training.
- The circumstances in which each of the job roles will need to communicate.

Knowing such things can enable the enterprise to make sure appropriate training is developed and made available and that the people performing these roles are supplied with the correct technology to allow them to carry out the Business Procedure Steps.

The previous three examples represent what are the most common use of Swim Lanes in Business Procedure modeling. However, Swim Lanes can be used to represent anything of significance to the enterprise. For example, if Swim Lanes are used to represent technologies, then the diagram would clearly display, not only the disparate technologies required for a Business Process, but also where interfaces would be required to link the technologies.

NOTE: For your convenience we have included a landscape version of the above diagram at the end of this subsection.

Landscape Diagram from Section 13.3 Swim Lanes as Job Roles

Swim Lanes as Job Roles

13.4. Swim Lanes vs Matrices

If the appropriate diagramming software is not available, it can be very time consuming to build different Business Procedure diagrams with Swim Lanes representing Business Departments, Locations, Job Roles, Technologies, etc. Because of this, the use of Swim Lanes is normally restricted to representing Business Departments or Job Roles.

	Log Fax or Letter	Verify Valid Order	Verify Registered Customer	Customer Credit Rating	Verify Valid Product	Verify Stock Status	Confirm Acceptance of Order	Authoriase Dispatch of Goods
Call Centre Clerk	✓	✓						
Call Centre Supervisor							✓	
Accounts Clerk			✓	✓				
Junior Storeman					✓	✓		✓

Matrix showing how the steps in a Business Procedure are spread across Job Roles.

Matrix Models are drawn with Business Functions on the one axis and any other relevant business element on the other axis to demonstrate the interrelationships. The example Matrix Model shown above has Business Functions across the top and Job Roles down the side.

13.5. Errors Using Swim Lanes

A common error in Business Procedure modeling occurs when a Business Procedure Step can occur in more than one department of an enterprise. In these circumstances, a common error is to draw the Business Procedure Step stretched across several Swim Lanes as in the following diagram.

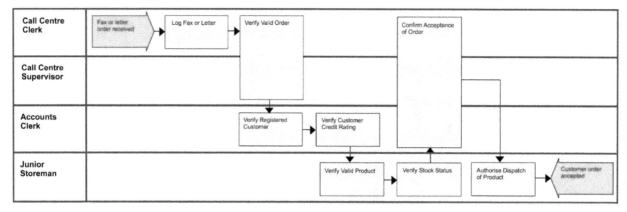

Modeling errors using swim lanes.

NOTE: For your convenience we have included a landscape version of the above diagram at the end of this subsection.

The problem with stretching the box across all Swim Lanes is that it is unclear exactly what the procedural flow is. For example, in the previous diagram, the steps 'Verify Valid Order' and 'Confirm Acceptance of Order' are both stretched across several Swim Lanes. What does this mean?

Is the step 'Verify Valid Order' carried out by **both** the Call Centre Clerk and the Call Centre Supervisor? If so, does this always happen or only under special circumstances? If so, what are the special circumstances?

The same questions must be asked for the step 'Confirm Acceptance of Order,' as the diagram suggests that this step is carried out by the Call Centre Clerk, the Call Centre Supervisor, and the Accounts Clerk!

So, what does happen in these circumstances? There are three possibilities:

1) The diagram is wrong, and each step is only ever carried out by one Job Role.
2) There are circumstances in which these steps are carried out by different job roles.
3) Anybody can carry out the steps.

If Option 1) previous is the case, then the diagram needs to be amended to correctly show which Job Role carries out the step in question.

If Option 2) is the case, then the diagram needs to be amended to show the circumstances in which a specific Job Role does the step.

If option 3) is the case, then drawing this Job Role Swim Lane view of the Business Procedure is a waste of time as it adds no value to the enterprise.

The same problem arises when a Business Procedure Step can happen in several departments. To know how the Business Procedure should flow, there must be known conditions that occur that cause the Business Procedure Step to be done in one department rather than another. Mapping these conditions on the Business Procedure diagram will make clear what these are.

The technique to use in these circumstances, whether a job role or a department, is to:

- Place an occurrence of the Business Procedure Step in question in each of the relevant Swim Lanes.
- Create a conditional branch at the Business Procedure Step preceding the Business Procedure Step in question.
- Write on each of the branches the condition that causes the Business Procedure Step to occur in the relevant department.

The following diagram shows how this is done.

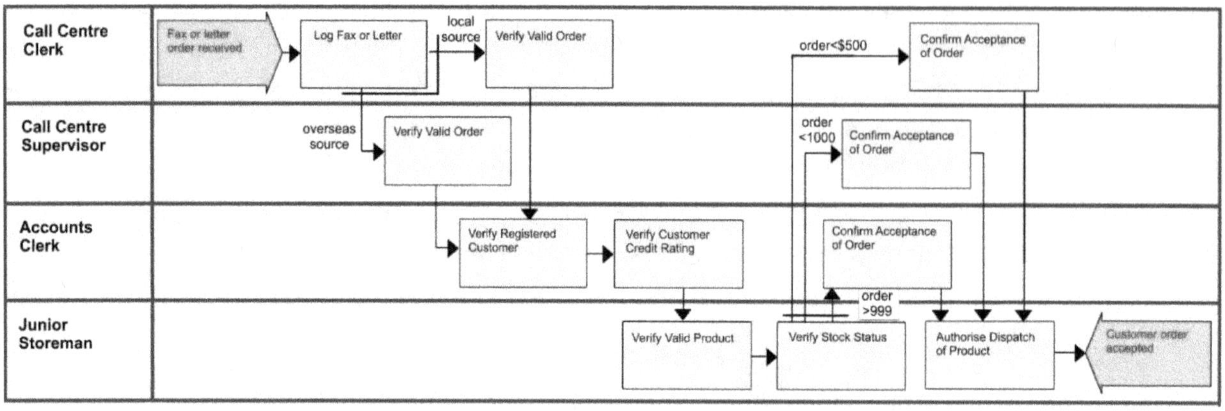

Swim lane modeling errors removed.

NOTE: For your convenience we have included a landscape version of the above diagram at the end of this subsection.

The above diagram removes the ambiguity that existed in the original diagram as to what happened after 'Log Fax or Letter' and shows the circumstances that cause the subsequent Business Procedure Step to be carried out by a specific Job Role.
The rule here is, 'Do not stretch Business Procedure Steps across Swim Lanes as to do so turns a Business Procedure Model into nothing more than an ambiguous sketch diagram.'

Landscape Diagrams from Section 13.5 Modeling errors using swim lanes

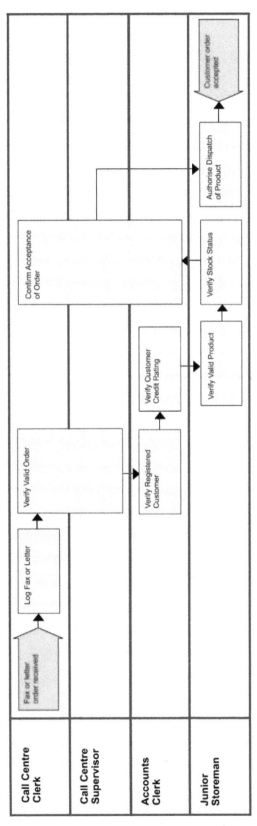

Modeling errors using swim lanes.

Landscape Diagrams from Section 13.5 Swim Lane modeling errors removed

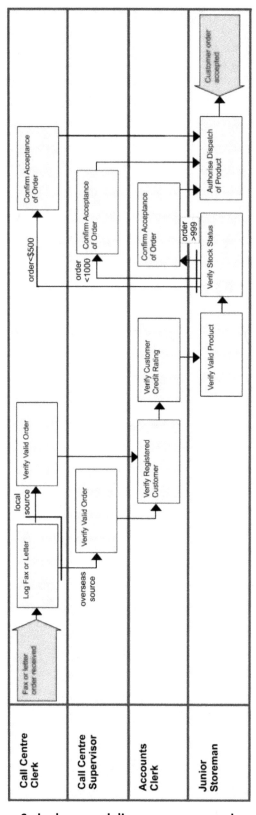

Swim lane modeling errors removed.

14. Worldview

Whenever Business Procedure models are drawn using Swim Lanes there are concepts called 'worldview' and 'management horizon' that bring a set of rules that allow these models to be drawn with greater clarity, simplicity, and rigor.

14.1. Definition: Worldview

To know what to include when building a Business Procedure Model, analysts must decide what 'world' they are in and where this 'world' starts and ends. This is called their 'worldview.' It must also be known what 'world' others are in and where those worlds start and end.

When there are multiple worlds, the analysts' is the 'primary world' and the way they view things is called the 'primary worldview.' Using the idea of 'worldview' makes Business Procedure models much more focused, relevant, and uncluttered.

For most Business Procedure models a worldview will be represented by a department in an enterprise, for example, the Sales Department, the Invoicing Department, etc. This is because that department wants to know and show how it interrelates to the rest of the enterprise with regard to a specific Business Procedure or, to put it another way, how its 'world' relates to the 'worlds' of others involved in the Business Procedure.

14.2. Definition: Management Horizon

Along with the concept of worldview goes the concept of 'Management Horizon.' This defines the parts of a Business Procedure over which management can be exercised (e.g., because they are done within the department) and those parts where it cannot be exercised (they are done by another department under different management or externally by a third party).

The concept of the 'Management Horizon' is important as there is a simple rule when modeling Business Procedures – 'you can only model Procedural flow that occurs within your management horizon.' At the management horizon the department will need to interface with another department or with a third party outside the enterprise. The management horizon rule applies to them too; they cannot model Procedural flow that occurs in your world as they have no control over it or responsibility for it.

The only objects that should appear on a Business Procedure model beyond the Management Horizon are entities in the other 'worlds' to which a Business Procedure Step passes information or from which it receives information.

14.3. Layout of the Diagram

Different 'Worlds' are represented on the Business Procedure diagrams by Swim Lanes. These Swim Lanes could be enterprise departments or locations.

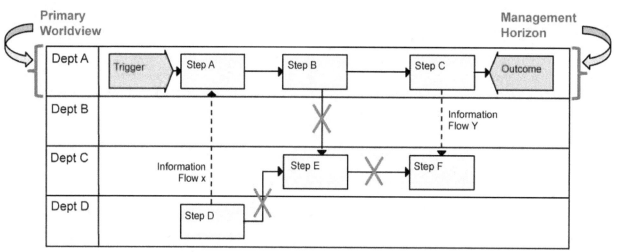

Diagram Showing Worldview and Management Horizon

The primary worldview should always be represented by the Swim Lane at the top of the Business Procedure diagram. The diagram above shows the primary worldview as Dept A. In this instance the Management Horizon coincides with the worldview, so the flow between Business Procedure Steps outside of Dept A should **not** be shown on the diagram.

The arrows going between Business Procedure Steps inside the management horizon are **flows of control** and are, as per our standards, shown as solid arrows. If information is being received from or passed to Business Procedure Steps outside of the management horizon these are shown as **dotted lines** and **must** be labeled with the name of the information, or data, that they represent.

The above diagram has several errors that can and should be avoided by using the concepts of Worldview and Management Horizon, these are:

Item	Error
Flows from Steps D to E and from E to F	These are flows of control that lie outside the management horizon of Dept A. For this reason, Dept A cannot say what the flows of control are and so they should not be shown on the diagram.
Flow from Step B to Step E	Control cannot be passed outside of the management horizon. This would mean losing control of the Business Procedure. Flow of information to other departments can be shown where it is important to show it as an integrated part of the Business Procedure, but not flow of control.
Dept B	There are no Business Procedure Steps in Dept B. This makes this Swim Lane superfluous, and it should be removed.

Removing the above errors from the diagram brings simplicity and clarity to the Business Procedure. Elegance, simplicity, and clarity are an essential part of Business Procedure modeling. The diagram below shows how these qualities are brought to the diagram by removing the listed errors.

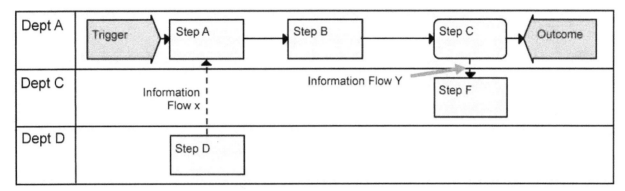

Flow errors removed from diagram.

The above Business Procedure has a lot more clarity and elegance. Business Procedure Step E has gone completely as it was only shown in the first place due to a modeling error.

14.4. More On Management Horizon

In the following diagram the Primary Worldview and the Management Horizon are represented by two different swim lanes.

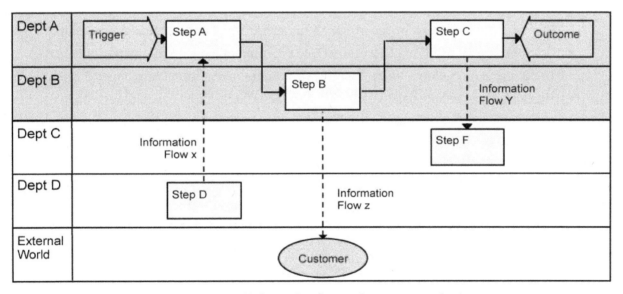

Business Process and information flow and management horizons

In the above diagram the Dept A is the primary worldview. The Management Horizon, which includes Dept A and Dept B, has been colored in. This is a very useful practice in both Business Process and Business Procedure modeling, as it makes it very clear where the Management Horizon starts and ends. The department representing the Primary Worldview should be shown at the top of the diagram. The other departments falling within the Management Horizon should be shown immediately underneath the swim lane for the Primary World view.

In the above diagram, even though Business Procedure Steps A, B and C are carried out by different departments, the flow of control between them can be shown because all these steps lie within the same Management Horizon.

Sometimes it is useful to show how information flows between a Business Procedure and the outside world. How this is done is shown in the above diagram with Information Flow Z going to the external entity 'Customer.'

However, these and all other information flows should only be included on a Business Procedure Model when they are needed to demonstrate something important to the understanding and execution of the Business Procedure.

When it needs to be known how information flows into, around, and out of an enterprise, the modeling technique to use is Information Flow Modeling.

> **This technique is described in detail in our book, IMM Information Flow Modeling available in paperback and ebook format from Amazon and Kindle.**

Interpreting Worldview Diagrams

A diagram based on worldviews can tell us a lot about a Business Procedure. The previous diagram tells us that:

- The Business Procedure involves four departments and the external world.
- The Business Procedure starts and ends in Department A.
- Flow of control passes from Department A to Department B on the completion of Step A.
- Flow of control passes from Department B to Department A on the completion of Step B.
- The Business Procedure is triggered by receipt of information from Department D.
- The Business Procedure passes information to the external entity of Customer at Step B
- The Business Procedure ends by passing information to Department C.

In a simple example like this Business Procedure, being able to tell all the above might seem quite trivial.

However, in large Business Procedures in large enterprises, being able to summarize a Business Procedure in these terms is essential in understanding how complex or fragmented it is in terms of the existing organization structure. If the Business Procedure involved a great number of departments this could present many communication problems. If many of the departments it spanned were outside of the management horizon of the primary worldview then the enterprise would have a major problem of control and coherence with the Business Procedure.

The passing of control between departments always presents a risk to Business Procedure continuity, which is of vital importance when implementing Workflow in an enterprise. For this reason, properly drawn Business Procedure diagrams are the cornerstone of any successful workflow project.

14.5. More on Data Flow

When the flow of information from a source outside the Primary Worldview is a Trigger for a Business Procedure, then the information flow should be shown on the diagram, as it is an integral part of the triggering.

Information flows can also be added at any point on a Business Procedure diagram if they add additional meaning.

Information flows should only be drawn between Business Procedure Steps in the Primary Worldview and other worldviews. They should *not* be drawn between Business Procedure Steps inside the Primary Worldview, as they could be confused with Business Procedure flow.

Business Procedure flows should NOT be labeled and made to 'double' as information flows. This is because information flow and Business Procedure flow are *entirely* different things and do not coincide.

If the primary objective is to show the flow of information between Business Procedure Steps, then the Business Procedure model is *not* a suitable vehicle. The Information Flow Diagram is the only business model that can effectively be used to demonstrate this.

> **For more details on Information Flow Diagrams see our book IMM Information Flow Modeling available in paperback and ebook from Amazon and Kindle.**

14.6. Rules for Swim Lanes

The following is a summary of the rules to follow whenever Business Procedure Models are drawn using Swim Lanes.

- All Triggers and Outcomes must lie within the Management. If any do not, then the Business Procedure is flawed.
- Flow of control can only be shown between Business Procedure Steps that are within the Management Horizon of the Primary Worldview.
- Information flows should only be shown between Business Procedure Steps that are in the Management Horizon and Business Procedure Steps that are outside of the Management Horizon.
- Information flows should never be shown between Business Procedure Steps within the Management Horizon.
- Business Procedure flows between objects outside of the Management Horizon should not be shown on the diagram.

Drawing diagrams that bring a focus to the 'world' within the Management Horizon avoids diagrams becoming so cluttered as to be unreadable.

It also allows managers to concentrate on the Business Procedure in their 'world' and make them aware of how many other worlds (over which they may have no control) they must interface with in order successfully to complete the Business Procedure.

It also highlights to these managers exactly where they lose management of the Business Procedure.

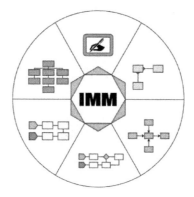

15. Mandatory Elements of a Business Procedure

For a model to formally qualify as a Business Procedure there is a minimum set of elements that it must contain. If any of these elements are missing then, whatever else it might be, the model in question is not a Business Procedure.

Item	Description
Trigger	A business event that initiates the Business Procedure. Every Business Procedure will have at least one, possibly several, Triggers. However, if a Business Procedure has a large number of Triggers, then it suggests that it is not a single Business Procedure but a compilation of several Business Procedures that need to be separated and rationalized.
Preferred Outcome	Achieving this outcome is the whole purpose of any Business Procedure. Every Business Procedure must have **a single, clearly defined, Preferred Outcome.** Without one it is not a Business Procedure. It is essential that the Preferred Outcome for a Business Procedure be completely aligned with Preferred Outcome for the Business Process on which the Business Procedure is based.
Non-Preferred Outcome	Each Business Procedure must have **at least one** (but may have several) Non-Preferred Outcome. This is a valid, though non-preferred, point at which to terminate the Business Procedure if the Preferred Outcome cannot be attained.
Business Procedure Steps	Each Business Procedure must have more than one step, otherwise it is not a Business Procedure. If it has only two or three steps, then it is a trivial Business Procedure and of little value to model.
Precedence or Business Procedure Flow	This defines the order in which Business Procedure Steps are to be executed and is indicated by an arrow going from one Business Procedure Step to another.
Branching	This defines alternative paths through the Business Procedure depending on some known condition, state, or value. Every Business Procedure should have at least one conditional branch to terminate the Business Procedure at the Non-Preferred Outcome if the Preferred Outcome cannot be attained.

15.1. Optional Elements of a Business Procedure

In addition to the above mandatory elements, a Business Procedure might also have any of the following elements defined for each of its steps.

Item	Description
Method	This describes: • The method by which each Business Procedure Step is to be carried out. • The valid Business Mechanism(s) for each step in the Business Process. • The logic for each step. • The responsibilities for execution of each step.
Controls	The controls required within a Business Procedure are defined for each step of the Business Procedure by defining: • The standards to be used when executing the step. • The risk associated with each step and the necessary mitigation. • The authorities required to execute the step.
Knowledge, Skills, and Competencies	This describes any relevant knowledge, skills, or competencies that the person carrying out the Business Procedure Step must have in order to be able to do it effectively and comply with all relevant guidelines, standards and legislation relating to the step.
Resources	This defines all resources that are required to carry out the Business Procedure Step. Depending on the industry, this could include: • Plant and equipment • Tools • Hardware • Applications • Technology
Evidence	This defines what information or physical evidence needs to be captured while executing each step in the Business Procedure to: • Ensure that the step is being properly executed. • Be able to demonstrate that it has been properly executed at any later date.

15.2. Work Instructions

When the step of a Business Procedure needs to be formally documented, this is done in what is called a Work Instruction. The format of a Work Instruction normally takes the form of a document naming the Business Procedure and, for each Business Procedure Step, the method, controls, knowledge, skills, competencies, resources, and evidence required for each step.

An example Work Instruction is shown in Section 18

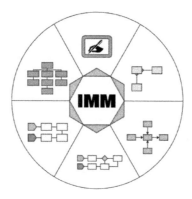

16. Detail for Business Procedure Elements

This section defines the complete detail that should be given for each attribute of each element of a Business Procedure, which are: Trigger, Preferred-Outcome, Non-Preferred Outcome, Business Procedure Step and Precedence.

16.1. Trigger

A Trigger is a Business Event to which the enterprise must respond by initiating a Business Process or a Business Procedure, as appropriate. The following information is required to fully describe a Trigger to a Business Procedure.

Attribute	Detail
Name*	Each Trigger should have a unique name. The name should begin with a *noun* and end with a *verb* in the *past participle*. For example, "Customer order received." Trigger names should be all lower case, except for the first letter and proper names or acronym initials, for example, "SLA agreed." SLA = Service Level Agreement.
Description	This should describe unambiguously what the Trigger is, for example, "The receipt of an order for the supply of products or services from a recognized customer. Orders can be received by email, phone, letter, or FAX."
Frequency	The frequency with which each Trigger occurs, for example, 500 times per day, 10 times per week, etc.
Response Required	This defines how quickly the Business Procedure Step being triggered must begin in response to the Triggering Event. This response time will be based on enterprise policy and might differ for each triggering Business Mechanism.
	For example, if a customer order is received by letter, fax or email a response time of 30 minutes might be quite acceptable. On the other hand, if the order is received by phone this would not be the case.

*Only the Name of the Trigger is shown on the Business Procedure diagram.

16.2. Preferred Outcome

The Preferred Outcome defines what a Business Procedure is intended to achieve in response to the Trigger that initiates it. The following information is required to fully describe a Preferred Outcome for a Business Procedure.

Attribute	Detail
Name*	Each Preferred Outcome must have a unique name. As with Triggers, the name should begin with a *noun* and end with a *verb* in the *past participle*. For example, "Customer order authorized." Outcome names should be all lower case, except for the initial letter and proper names or initials, for example, "SLA agreed" (SLA = Service Level Agreement).
Description	This should expand on the name of the Preferred Outcome and unambiguously describe what it is. For the Outcome "Customer order authorized" an appropriate description would be: "This outcome indicates that a customer order has been received and gone through all the stages of processing and authority given to dispatch the products ordered."
Frequency	The frequency with which each Outcome occurs, for example, 500 times per day, 10 times per week, etc. This frequency may be less than that for the Trigger as not all orders that are received will be authorized.

*Only the name of the Preferred Outcome is shown on the Business Procedure diagram.

16.3. Non-Preferred Outcome

This is a desirable but non-preferred outcome to a Business Procedure if the Preferred Outcome cannot be attained. The following information is required to fully describe a Non-Preferred Outcome for a Business Procedure.

Attribute	Detail
Name*	Each Non-Preferred Outcome must have a unique name. As with Preferred Outcomes, the name should begin with a noun and end with a *verb* in the past participle. For example, "Customer order rejected." Non-Preferred Outcome names should be all lower case, except for the first letter and proper names or acronym initials, for example, "SLA rejected" (SLA = Service Level Agreement). The name might also describe, as far as is possible in few words, the reason the Non-Preferred Outcome occurred, for example, "Order rejected - bad debt," "Order rejected – no stock." As in these examples, the condition can be added after the past participle.
Description	This should expand on the name of the Non-Preferred Outcome and describe unambiguously what the Non-Preferred Outcome is and the circumstances that would bring it about. For the Non-Preferred Outcome "Order rejected - bad debt" a suitable description would be: "A customer credit status was checked, and the customer found to be a 'bad debt' as defined under current credit policy. The order was rejected for this reason."

Attribute	Detail
Frequency	The frequency with which each Non-Preferred Outcome occurs, for example, 100 times per day, 5 times per week, etc. This frequency will be less than that for the Trigger as it is hoped that few if any orders will be rejected.

*Only the name of the Non-Preferred Outcome is shown on the Business Procedure diagram.

16.4. Business Procedure Step

Business Procedure Steps are the actions or activities that bring about the results that the Business Procedure is intended to achieve. The following information is required to fully describe a Business Procedure Step.

Attribute	Detail
Name*	Each Business Procedure Step must have a unique name. This name will be that of the Business Process Step on which the Business Procedure is based. When a Business Procedure Step represents one of several Business Mechanisms for implementing a Business Process Step, then the name should reflect both the Business Process Step and the Business Mechanism, for example, 'Log Fax Orders,' 'Establish Nature of Telephone Call,' etc.
Description	The description for the Business Procedure Step will be exactly the same as that for the Business Process Step that it is implementing, except when the Business Procedure Step is implementing a particular Business Mechanism. When this is the case, then the description must define fully all the relevant logic, business rules, performance metrics, key performance indicators (KPIs), etc. for the Business Procedure Step.
Frequency	The frequency with which the Business Procedure Step occurs, for example, 500 times per day, 10 times per week, etc. Again, this might be the same as that for the Business Process Step it is implementing or might be different in order to reflect the frequency with which a particular Business Mechanism is implemented.

*Only the name of the Business Procedure Step is shown on the Business Procedure diagram.

16.5. Swim Lane

When a Business Procedure is drawn using swim lanes, the following information is required to describe them fully.

Attribute	Detail
Name*	A unique name for the Swim Lane, for example, 'Accounts Department,' 'Personnel Department.'
Description	A description that expands on the name to avoid ambiguity, for example 'Accounts department at head office, excluding Cash Office.'

*Only the name of the Swim Lane is shown on the Business Procedure diagram.

The definitions of those attributes for Business Procedure elements that will not appear on the Business Procedure diagram should be contained in supporting documentation or in a CASE Tool if one is being used.

17. Business Process and Procedure Modeling Conventions

For Business Processes and Business Procedure Models to be correct and unambiguous, strict modeling conventions need to be known and applied when building them. This Section describes in detail all the elements of a Business Process and all of the conventions needed in order to model Business Processes and Business Procedures to a consistently high quality.

Although the conventions are described below in terms of how they apply to Business Processes, the rules are the same for Business Procedures. The only difference is that in IMM the steps in a Business Process are shown as 'rounded boxes' ⬭ and those in a Business Procedure as rectangles ▭.

17.1. Business Process Flow

This Section describes the ways in which control can flow through a Business Process and shows how all these forms are drawn on Business Process diagrams.

Adding Triggering to Precedence

In item 4) above it was stated that "B can begin at any appropriate time after A has finished". In some circumstances we may need to be more specific and show this on the Business Process diagram. How do we do this?

Let us look at an example to demonstrate what we mean:

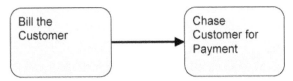

This diagram tells us four things:

1) 'Bill the Customer' occurs before 'Chase Customer for Payment.'
2) On completion of 'Bill the Customer' control passes to 'Chase Customer for Payment.'
3) 'Chase Customer for Payment' cannot begin until 'Bill the Customer' has finished.
4) 'Chase Customer for Payment' can begin at any appropriate time after 'Bill the Customer' has finished.

So, when do we chase the customer for payment? In item 3) we stated that on completion of 'Bill the Customer' control passes to 'Chase Customer for Payment'. Does that mean that 'Chase Customer for Payment' must start immediately? Not necessarily! It is up to the people responsible for the Business Process Step 'Chase Customer for Payment' to decide what the appropriate time is to do this. This will be defined by the prevailing company policy and will be embedded in the Business Function logic for the Business Function 'Chase Customer for Payment.' This Business Functions logic must be reflected in the Business Process Step used to carry out the Business Function.

However, this logic is not apparent on the Business Process diagram. So, we need to ask, "Does the triggering need to be shown on the Business Process diagram" and, if the answer is 'yes,' "How do we show it?"

Let us suppose that company policy states that all customers should be chased for payment immediately that the Payment Due Date has been reached. How would we show this on the Business Process diagram? The answer is to add a Triggering Event or Trigger to the Business Process that, merged with the completion of the previous Step, triggers 'Chase Customer for Payment,' as shown below:

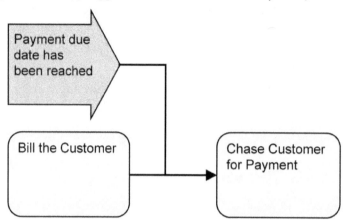

Notice that the arrow from the Trigger is merged with the arrow from the preceding Step. This structure tells us that:

- On completion of 'Bill the Customer' control passes to 'Chase Customer for Payment,' but only when the Trigger 'Payment due date has been reached' has occurred.

- 'Chase Customer for Payment' cannot begin until 'Bill the Customer' has finished and the 'Payment due date has been reached' has occurred.

- 'Chase Customer for Payment' can begin at any appropriate time after 'Bill the Customer' has finished and the Event 'Payment due date has been reached' has occurred.

So, in summary, if the triggering of a Business Process Step needs to be shown on a Business Process diagram more specifically than 'at any appropriate time' then a Triggering Event should be added before that Business Process Step and merged, as appropriate, with the Business Process flow from preceding Business Process Step(s).

Business Process Step to Business Process Step

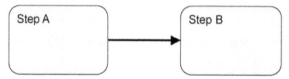

The most common form of Business Process flow is going from one Business Process Step to another Business Process Step, as shown in the above diagram. The arrow going from Step A to Step B tells us several things:

1) In the context of the Business Process being modeled, A is carried out before B.

2) In the context of the Business Process being modeled on completion of A control passes to B.

3) In the context of the Business Process being modeled, B cannot begin until A has finished.

4) In the context of the Business Process being modeled, B can begin at any appropriate time after A has finished.

The phrase *'in the context of the Business Process being modeled'* is used to point out that the Business Process flow shown between the objects in a particular Business Process diagram can be thought of as being valid and true **ONLY** in the <u>context of the Business Process that the diagram represents</u>.

Regarding Business Process Step A and Business Process Step B, it is possible, and probable, that in other Business Processes these two steps might be related in an entirely different manner.

For this reason, each statement in the following text defining Business Process flow should be thought of as beginning with the phrase *'in the context of the Business Process being modeled.'*

When checking the correctness of a Business Process model with key members of the enterprise It is a very useful practice to initially state the relationships between the Steps as expressed in 1) and 2) and then ask for verification of the relationship by restating it as expressed in 3) and 4) above – these are known as the 'reverse form'. The reason for this is that the relationship as stated by the direct form, in 1) and 2) above always seems self-evident. However, when people are presented with the statements in the reverse form, they are made to re-think their original assumptions.

They ask themselves: 'Is it *really* true that B *cannot* begin before A is complete?' or 'can B *really* begin *any time* after A has finished?' The responses to these questions often brings changes that significantly improve the Business Process being modeled. The term 'improve' is an understatement as they often change the Business Process from being wrong to being right!

In all forms of analysis asking the reverse form of a question is a powerful technique for validating the direct form. People will often quickly agree with the direct form and then revise their opinion when presented with the reverse form.

Trigger to Business Process Step

Business events that start up Business Processes are called 'Triggers.'

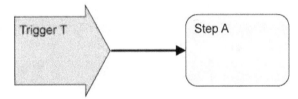

The above is a segment of a Business Process that tells us two things:

- The occurrence of the Trigger T starts up Business Process Step A and, by doing that, the whole Business Process.
- In the context of the Business Process being modeled, Business Process Step A cannot begin until the Trigger T has occurred.

The relationship between a Trigger and a Business Process Step differs from that between a Business Process Step and another Business Process Step in that control does not pass from the Trigger to the Business Process Step. Triggers do not have 'control' of a Business Process; rather they initiate a Business Process Step, which then has control.

Business Process Step to Outcome

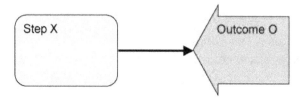

The previous Business Process flow tells us two things:

- The completion of Step X results in Outcome O. Events arising as the result of the completion of Business Process Steps are called Outcomes.

- Outcome O cannot occur before Step X has been completed.

Again, the relationship between a Business Process Step and an Outcome differs from that between a Business Process Step and a Business Process Step in that control does not pass from the Business Process Step to the Outcome. As with Triggers, Outcomes do not have 'control' of the Business Process; they end the need for control because they end the Business Process.

17.2. Triggering

The term 'Triggering' is often incorrectly used to describe all arrows linking objects on a Business Process diagram, which they do not. There are three different types of linking with arrows that can occur in a Business Process and only one of them can be accurately described as triggering.

Direct Triggering

All Business Processes must be 'triggered' before they can begin. That is, something must happen, an event must occur, that starts the Business Process. The only thing that can validly start up a Business Process is a Triggering Event. An Event that causes a Business Process Step (and hence a Business Process) to be triggered is called a Trigger. All Triggers require a Business Process Step to be started as the result of their occurrence. If an Event does not require a Business Process Step to be started, then it is not a Trigger!

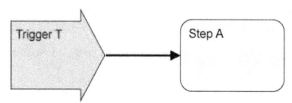

The above diagram shows an Event triggering to a Business Process Step. This Event is a Trigger. This is the only type of direct 'triggering' that occurs in a Business Process.

How soon after the Trigger T occurs must the Step A begin? Immediately? Soon? Response times cannot be stated in these vague terms. They need to be stated in exact terms, for example 'within 10 seconds', 'within three minutes', etc. The response time is part of the definition of the Trigger (see section 16.1)

Precedence vs Triggering

Precedence is often mistaken for triggering. It is often mistakenly assumed that if two Steps on a Business Process diagram are joined by an arrow that the Step at the source of the arrow 'triggers' the Step at the point of the arrow.

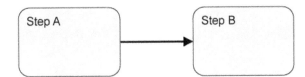

As was explained previously, an arrow going from Business Process Step A to Business Process Step B tells us four things:

1) A is carried out before B.

2) On completion of A control passes to B.

3) B cannot begin until A has finished.

4) B can begin at any appropriate time after A has finished

All the above statements are about precedence. None of them tells us that 'A triggers B,' so precedence is NOT triggering.

Internal and External Triggers

Triggers are sometimes referred to as 'internal' and 'external.' However, it is not always easy to differentiate these. This is why in IMM™ there are clear definitions of what is meant by 'Internal Trigger' and by 'External Trigger.'

Internal Trigger

An Internal Trigger is an Event that *occurs within the enterprise* to which the enterprise must respond by initiating a Business Process.

An Internal Trigger may have an occurrence outside the enterprise as its source, but it is not until the enterprise becomes aware of the occurrence internally that it can respond to it; by which time it has become an internal Event!

For example, an external event to which a utility company may need to respond is a customer moving house. The customer could move house without telling the company. The company would remain unaware of this external event and no Business Process would be triggered.

This is the case for most external events. They do not actually trigger Business Processes within the enterprise because the enterprise is unaware that the event has occurred.

But what happens if the customer moving house tells the utility company about the move? Once the enterprise has been told about the move then appropriate action can be triggered within the enterprise. But the event is now an internal Event! This is a very important distinction to make in order to ensure that Business Processes get triggered properly.

The external event that the utility company needed to know about was that a customer had moved house. The Event to which it could respond was the notification of the move by the customer. Using the IMM™ naming conventions for Triggers this would become 'Customer house move notified.'

External Trigger

There are few, if any, external events that will trigger Business Processes in an enterprise because the enterprise will be unaware that they have occurred.

In some enterprises, however, it might be essential to be aware of such events and respond to them without being notified. The only way to achieve this is to have Business Functions that monitor the world externally and to watch for and identify occurrences that are significant to the enterprise.

Financial institutions have many such Business Functions that monitor stock prices, market trends, etc. to identify the occurrence of events to which they must react by buying, selling, etc, as appropriate.

Outcomes and Triggering

Outcomes are not triggered. They are a state that arises as the result of the execution of a series of Business Process Steps. An arrow from a Business Process Step to an Outcome indicates that it was the last Business Process Step that needed to be executed to arrive at the Outcome.

17.3. Business Process Flow and 'Dependency'

Business Process flow is sometimes referred to as 'dependency.'

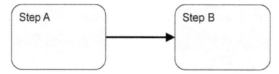

When speaking in terms of dependency the above diagram would tell us:

- Step B is dependent on Step A
- Step B resolves the dependency between A and B

IMM™ does not use the term 'dependency' as it is a concept that is not intuitive or self-evident and, as such, is open to misinterpretation.

17.4. Multiple Flows

Multiple Business Process flows is where several arrowheads arrive at a single object on a Business Process diagram.

Exclusive Multiple Flows

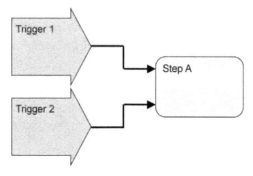

The above diagram shows an 'exclusive multiple Business Process flow,' normally called an 'exclusive flow.' This tells us three things:

- The occurrence of EITHER Trigger 1 OR Trigger 2 will initiate Step A.
- Step A cannot begin until EITHER Trigger 1 OR Trigger 2 has occurred.
- Step A will be triggered either by Trigger 1 **OR** by Trigger 2 but **NEVER** by *both*. This structure is referred to as an **'implied arc'** and will be explained in more detail (see section 17.8).
-

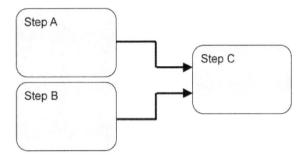

The above diagram also shows an exclusive multiple Business Process flow. This tells us that:

- The completion of EITHER Step A OR Step B will allow Step C to begin.
- Step C cannot begin until EITHER Step A or Step B has finished.
- Step C can begin either when Step A OR by Step B has been completed but NEVER by both. Again, this structure is an 'implied arc' and will be explained in more detail (see section 17.8).

Merged Multiple Flows

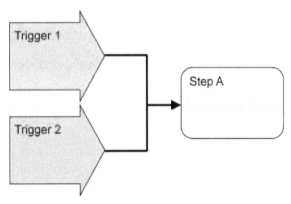

The above diagram segment shows a 'merged multiple Business Process flow,' normally called a merged flow. This tells us that:

- The occurrence of **BOTH** Trigger 1 **AND** Trigger 2 are required to initiate Step A.
- Step A cannot begin until **BOTH** Triggers have occurred.

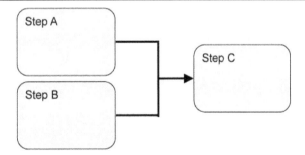

The above diagram segment also shows a merged flow. This tells us that:

- The completion of BOTH Step A AND Step B are required before Step C can begin.
- Step C cannot begin until BOTH Step A AND Step B have been completed.

Mixed Multiple Flows

Multiple flows can be a combination of any number of Business Process Steps or Triggers.

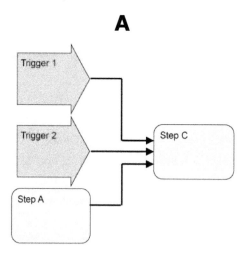

Example A above is an exclusive flow that tells us that:

- Step C can begin after the occurrence of Trigger 1 OR the occurrence of Trigger 2 OR the completion of Business Process Step A.

- Step C cannot begin until Trigger T1 has occurred OR Trigger T2 has occurred OR Business Process Step A has finished.

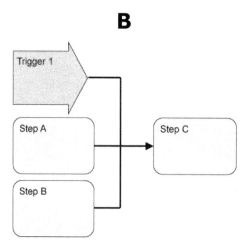

Example B above is a merged flow that tells us:

- Step C can begin after the occurrence of Trigger 1 AND the completion of Steps A AND B.

- Step C cannot begin until Trigger 1 has occurred AND Steps A AND B have been completed.

17.5. Compound Flows

Exclusive flows and merged flows can be combined into what are called compound flows to achieve the necessary structures for all types of Business Process.

A

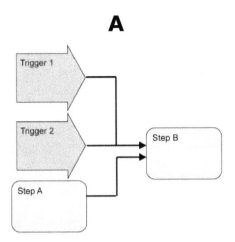

Example A above shows that:

- Business Process Step B can begin EITHER after the occurrence of Trigger 1 AND Trigger 2 OR after the completion of Business Process Step A.

- Step B cannot begin until both Trigger 1 AND Trigger 2 have occurred OR until Business Process Step A has finished.

B

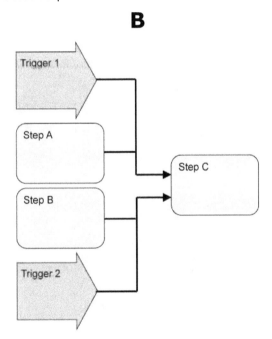

Example B above shows that:

- Business Process Step C can begin EITHER after the occurrence of Trigger 1 AND the completion of Business Process Step A OR the completion of Business Process Step B AND the occurrence of Trigger 2.

- Business Process Step C cannot begin until Trigger 1 occurs AND Business Process Step A has finished OR Business Process Step B has finished AND Trigger 2 has occurred.

17.6. Branching

In real life, Business Processes will not be as simple and straightforward as those we have dealt with so far. Most Business Processes will include 'branches' where the route through the Business Process splits. There are two types of branch: unconditional and conditional.

Unconditional Branch

An unconditional branch occurs when steps of a Business Process can be carried out simultaneously as shown below.

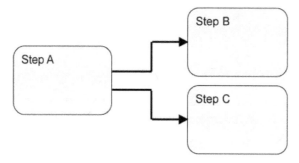

In the above *unconditional branch*, after Business Process Step A has finished, control is passed to both Business Process Step B and Business Process Step C. This is not an 'either/or' situation, as **BOTH** Step B and Step C can begin after the completion of Step A. For this reason, it is better to draw the diagram as follows, where the arrows leaving Business Process Step A have been merged into one.

A real-life example of an unconditional branch is shown below:

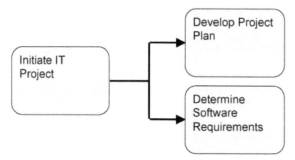

In the above example, 'Develop Project Plan' **AND** 'Determine Software Requirements' can **BOTH** start after 'Initiate IT Project' has finished.

Conditional Branch

A conditional branch is where the route through the Business Process is determined by the occurrence of some state or value.

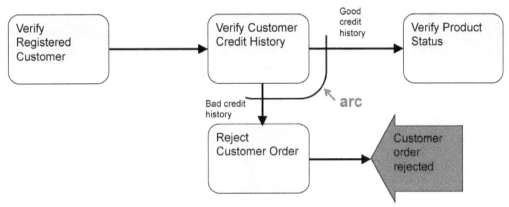

In the above example, if the customer has a good credit rating, then we proceed with the order and verify the product status. If the credit rating is bad, then we reject the order and end the Business Process. Because the route taken is based on some condition being satisfied this is called a 'conditional' branch.

Because the conditions being met are mutually exclusive, i.e., the customer must *either* have a good credit rating *or* a bad one, the flows leaving the decision-making Business Process Step are also said to be mutually exclusive. The drawing convention in IMM™ for showing mutually exclusive flows leaving a Business Process is a line drawn across the flows. This line is called an **'arc.'**

The Outcome 'Customer order rejected' is a **Non-Preferred Outcome**.

The evaluation carried out by a Business Process Step can result in any number of (two or more) predefined states, so any number of flows can be included in an arc.

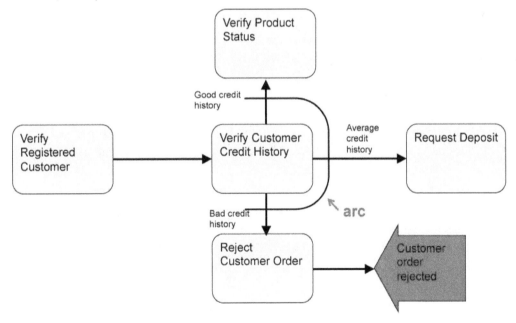

In the example above the Business Process Step 'Verify Customer Credit History' evaluates the customer's credit record and classes it as one of three possible status, 'good,' 'average or 'bad.' Each of these status will pass control to a different Business Process Step after the completion 'Verify Customer Credit History.'

The use of the **Arc** in Business Process Modeling is a very convenient way to model two or more conditional branches leaving a Business Process Step. Unfortunately, not all modeling software includes the arc. When this is the case, the valid options need to be modeled in a binary or 'yes/no' structure, as shown below.

This 'binary' approach had its roots in computer flow-charting. Although it is exact, it is far less elegant than the arc structure, which is just as exact.

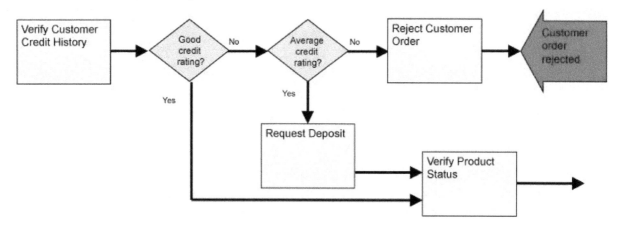

Binary branching as sometimes drawn in Business Procedures

There are four main disadvantages to this binary approach:

- It adds unnecessary symbols to the diagram. The Business Process Step 'Verify Customer Credit History' has tested for the appropriate statuses and yet this testing must be shown again in the binary boxes.

- All situations must be reduced to binary format. This has advantages when designing the algorithm for a computer program but offers none when modeling a Business Process or a Business Procedure.

- The integrity of Business Process models is maintained at a high level by the rule that all steps in a Business Process should be Elementary Business Functions (EBFs) from the Business Function Model (BFM) for the enterprise in question. Binary decision boxes such as, 'Good Credit Rating?,' 'Average Credit Rating?,' etc. are not EBFs and so break this crucial integrity rule.

- This approach detracts from the elegance of the Business Process model. This desire for elegance is not just an aesthetic thing. A Business Process diagram is a visual aid to understanding a Business Process and, as such, should be pleasing to the eye. If it is, it will also be easier to understand and will reduce confusion and ambiguity.

For these reasons IMM™ does not use or advocate the use of binary decision boxes in Business Process or Business Procedure diagrams.

17.7. More Complex Business Process Flows

In this section we will look at more complex Business Process flows and describe what they mean.

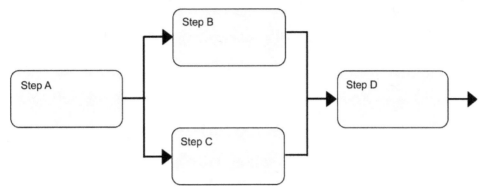

The above diagram tells us:

- When Business Process Step A has finished control passes BOTH to Step B and to Step C.
- Step B cannot start until Step A has finished.
- Step C cannot start until Step A has finished.
- When BOTH Step B and Step C have finished control passes to Step D.
- Step D cannot start until BOTH Step B and Step C have finished.

An example of such a construction in real life is shown below.

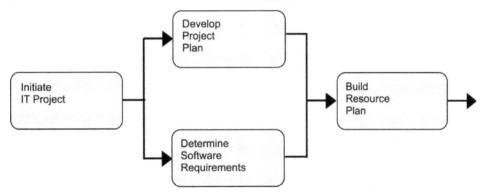

In the above example:

- When 'Initiate IT Project' has finished control passes to BOTH 'Develop Project Plan' AND 'Determine Software Requirements.'
- NEITHER of these can begin until 'Initiate IT Project' has finished.
- Either of them can begin at any appropriate time after 'Initiate IT Project' has finished.
- 'Build Resource Plan' cannot begin until BOTH 'Develop Project Plan' and 'Determine Software Requirements' have been completed.

This makes sense because:

- Before the resource plan can be built the stages and activities of the project plan need to be known.
- The required resource types (i.e., what people with what skills) cannot be determined until the type of software to be developed has been established.

The following example shows a more complex conditional branching than our previous examples.

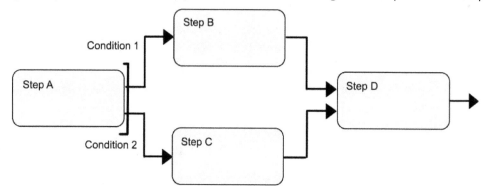

The above example contains two arcs.

- The arc across the flows leaving Step A shows that on completion of Step A EITHER Step B OR Step C can start but NOT both.

- The separate arrows going into Step D are an 'implied arc' (see section 17.8 for more detail) meaning that only one of the flows will occur, i.e., Step D can begin EITHER after Step B has finished OR after Step C has finished.

The following construction can be summarized as, "From an initial Step A, Step D can only begin when both Step B **AND** Step C have finished." The sequence of Step B and Step C does not matter. They can occur at the same time or at different times.

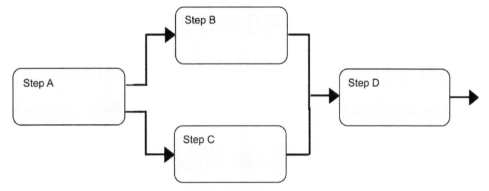

Another way to draw the flows out of A is as shown below.

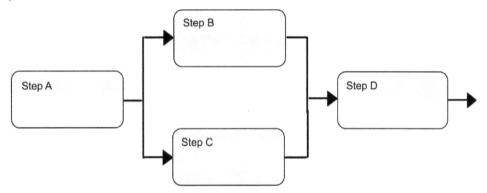

Here the two flows have been merged as they leave Step A and then split before they arrive at Step B and Step C. Both methods are equally valid but, for consistency, they ought not be mixed on the same diagram.

17.8. Implied Arc

The **implied arc** is something to be especially aware of as, although it is not physically represented on the Business Process diagram, it always applies to the Business Process logic.

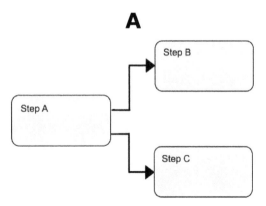

In **Example A** above, when Business Process Step A has finished both Step B and Step C may begin. This is shown by two arrows leaving A, one going to Step B the other going to Step C.

B

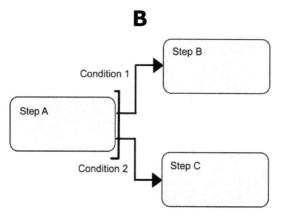

In **Example B** above, when Business Process Step A has finished **_EITHER_** Step B **_OR_** Step C may begin, depending on some condition, but not both. The flows leaving Step A and going to Step B and Step C are **_mutually exclusive_**. This is explicitly shown by the arc drawn across the two arrows.

Because flows **_leaving_** a Business Process Step may or may not be mutually exclusive it is necessary physically to draw an arc on the flows to indicate when they are.

This is not true for Business Process flows **_entering_** a Business Process Step as these are **<u>ALWAYS MUTUALLY EXCLUSIVE</u>**! Because the arc does not need to be drawn it is referred to as an **'implied arc.'**

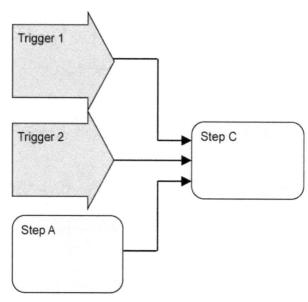

In both the examples above and following **_only one_** of the Business Process flows entering Step C will occur at any one time.

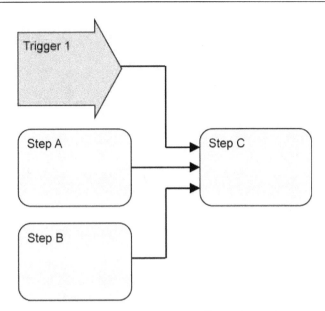

The reason flows entering a Business Process Step are mutually exclusive is to ensure that, on any one pass through a Business Process, that a Business Process Step will be executed **in only one way at each pass**. This ensures that a Business Process Step cannot be inadvertently carried out repeatedly. This is important for all Business Process Steps, as to do so would, at the very least, waste time and is inefficient. However, it could also cost the enterprise money if Business Process Steps such as 'Pay Creditors' were inadvertently carried out repeatedly!

17.9. Business Process Flows and Looping

In all the Business Process examples so far, control flowed from left to right through the Business Process. This is not always the case. Sometimes, control must be passed back to a previous point in the Business Process. This usually happens when a particular state is required to exist before control can pass on to a subsequent Business Process Step.

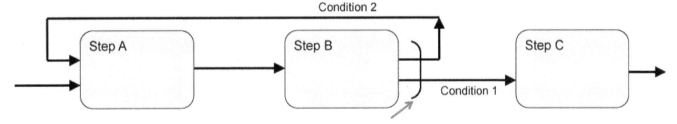

In the above example, when Step B has been completed, if Condition 1 exists then control passes to Step C, if not, control is passed back to Step A.

Step A is repeated, followed by Step B. The test for Condition 1 is repeated. Again, if Condition 1 exists, control is passed to Step C, otherwise it passes back to Step A.

This looping will continue until Condition 1 exists, when control will pass to Step C and then on to other steps in the Business Process.

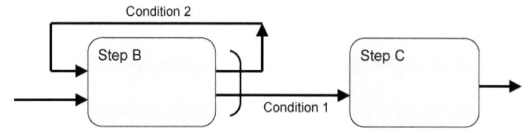

The above diagram represents what is called a 'trivial loop.' This structure is saying that Step B is carried out and a test made to see if Condition 1 exists. If it does, then control passes to Step C. If it does not, then Step B is carried out again. In other words, Step B is carried out over and over until Condition 1 exists.

The fact is that every Step in a Business Process could be drawn with such looping, as it is only when a particular condition exists that a Step can be said to be complete, and control passed on to the next Step. This is why this is called a 'trivial loop.' It is a loop that happens internally in every Business Process Step, and which need not (indeed ought not) be shown as it simply adds unnecessary complexity.

It is only when a particular condition exists, or fails to exist, which would require control to be passed back to a Step other than the current Step that looping ought to be explicitly shown.

17.10. 'Illegal' Structures

There are some arrangements of objects and Business Process flows that are not permissible in Business Process diagrams. This is because they are illogical or would create inconsistencies in the execution of the Business Process that would result in the output of the Business Process being unpredictable. This section lists the most common of these 'illegal' structures and explains the rules involved to help avoid building others.

17.11. Illegal Associations

Multiple Associations

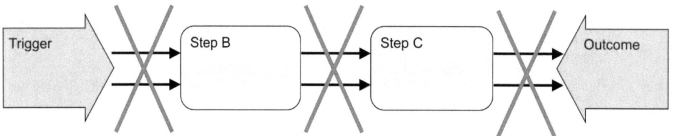

Multiple associations refers to the drawing of two (or more) Business Process flows between the same two objects on the diagram. There can only ever be **one** Business Process flow between a pair of objects in a Business Process. Any more than one would result in an indeterminate outcome.

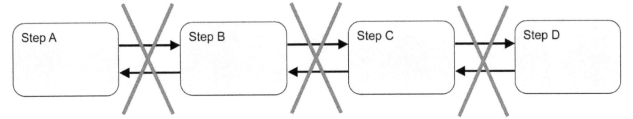

The multiple associations above would result in deadlock for the Business Process. The arrows specify Step B cannot begin until Step A has been completed, also that Step A cannot begin until Step B has been completed - deadlock. The same deadlock exists between steps B, C and D.

Trigger to Outcome

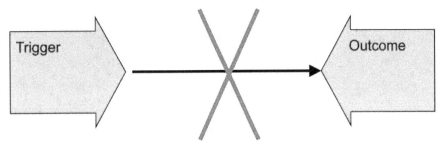

A Trigger cannot be linked directly to an Outcome. There are two main reasons for this:

- Events are Events, they do not trigger Events, they trigger Business Process Steps.
- The basic definition for an Outcome defines it as arising as the result of the execution of one or more Business Process steps so it must be preceded by a Business Process Step.

Business Process Step to Trigger

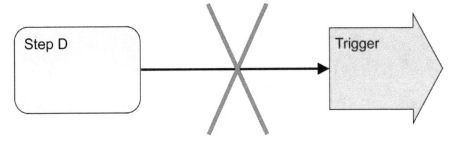

A Business Process Step cannot precede a Trigger. A Trigger is always the first object in a Business Process.

Outcome to Business Process Step

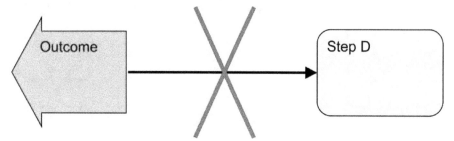

An Outcome cannot precede a Business Process Step. The definition of an Outcome tells us that it terminates a Business Process, so no Business Process Step can follow it.

Outcome to Trigger

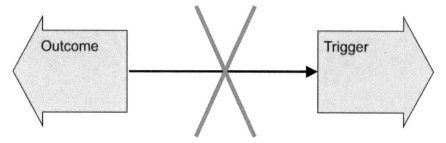

An Outcome cannot be linked to or precede a Trigger as shown in the previous diagram. Triggers and Outcomes can have special relationships that are discussed in detail in Section 12.2

Triggers and Arcs

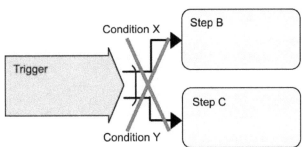

An arc cannot be placed across the flows leaving a Trigger as in the above diagram. A Trigger cannot evaluate situations and decide what action to take; only a Business Process Step can do that.

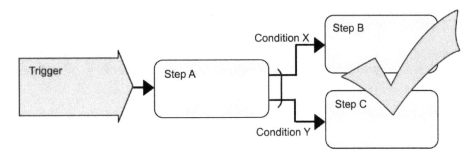

So, if an evaluation is needed immediately after a Trigger occurs, then the first step in the Business Process should be an evaluation Business Process Step with an arc across the flows leaving it, as shown in the previous diagram.

17.12.   Violation of Implied Arc

The Implied Arc Rule tells us that a Business Process Step **cannot** be triggered by more than one Business Process flow at any one time, even if it has more than one flow going to it.

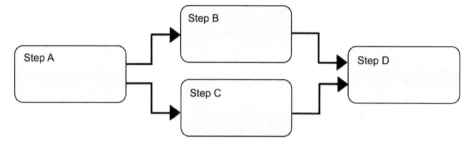

Following the implied arc rule, In the above diagram, control will be passed to Step D **either** by Step B **or** Step C. Yet the diagram shows us that on the completion of Step A, **both** Step B and Step C will be carried out, which would result in both of them passing control to Step D.

This obviously illogical structure is a modeling error that can happen if the principle of the **implied arc** is forgotten (see section 17.8 for more detail). The diagram needs to be altered to one of the two following structures.

The following diagrams solve the inconsistency of the previous diagram.

The first diagram has introduced an arc to ensure that the flows to Step B and Step C are mutually exclusive. **Either** Step B **or** Step C will occur, depending on some condition at Step A, so the implied arc at Step D is satisfied.

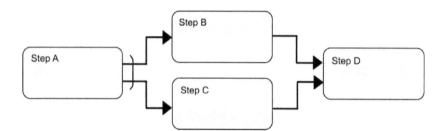

The second diagram shows that both Step B and Step C occur after Step A. The solution here is to merge the flows from Step B and Step C to Step D, showing that Step D can occur only after both Step B **and** Step C have finished.

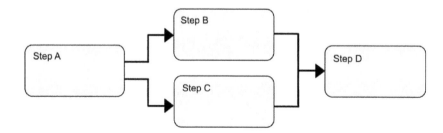

The violation of the implied arc is less easy to spot when it happens 'from a distance' as in the following diagram. Here, on completion of Step X, both Step Y and Step D can begin. But Step D can also occur on the completion of Step B or Step C. This means that Step D can occur twice!

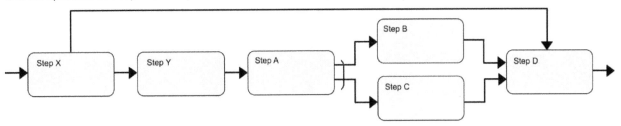

Remembering the rule that **all flows entering a Business Process Step are mutually exclusive** will help to avoid these errors.

The only time a Business Process Step can validly be triggered more than once during a Business Process is through looping (see section 17.9). But the rule on implied arcs still applies in looping.

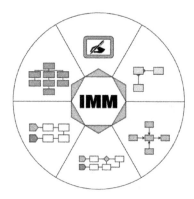

18. Example of Work Instruction

Pan Euro Credit Union
Work Instruction

Procedure Name: Validating Applications for Loans

Purpose	To ensure that all requests for loans are processed according to the existing standards and guidelines of the organisation. To maximise the overall funds lent without exposing Pan Euro Credit Union to unacceptable risk.

Procedure Step	Receive Applications for Loans
Mechanisms	Valid applications can be received by four valid channels, letter, fax, email and website form. This Work Instruction relates only to those received by letter of fax.
Method	When a letter or fax is received in the Loans Office it must be stamped and with the date and time of receipt as this a) is a legal requirements and b) it will start the clock running with regard to delivery of service to the applicant.
Responsibilities	This initial processing of these applications is the responsibility of the Mail Clerk under the supervision of the Loans Office Manager.
Standards	Only plain white A4 fax paper is to be used.
Risks	FAX machines must be checked for paper stock every 15 minutes to prevent inadvertent stoppages.
Authorities	If anything occurs that require the Mail Clerk to deviate from this Work Instruction, then he/she must seek permission from the Loans Office Manager before doing so and the variation to the Procedure must be documented in the Loans Office Operations Log.
Knowledge, Skills, Competencies	No special knowledge, competencies or skills are required for this task.
Resources	Only mail arriving in the 'Loans In' mail tray and faxes arriving on Fax machines labelled 'Loans Only' are to be processed following this Work Instruction.
Evidence	Each letter and fax must have the date and time stamp applied to the top right hand corner using stamp labelled LTAD. The applied stamp must be initialled by the Mail Clerk.

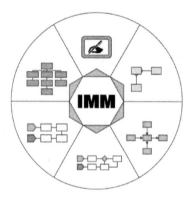

19. About the Authors

Discover the works of John Owens and Pam Walton, acclaimed thought leaders, speakers, writers, consultants, and mentors. With an impressive array of expertise, they are revolutionizing the world of Business Architecture Modeling. Renowned worldwide for their innovative approaches, John and Pam have spearheaded projects in a diverse range of industries spanning the globe. Their international reputation as highly skilled specialists precedes them, with a successful record in the UK, Ireland, Europe, Australia, and New Zealand.

Their unique ability to train, coach, and mentor individuals, regardless of technical background, sets them apart. Through their guidance, both technical and non-technical professionals gain the skills to become highly competent analysts and business architects.

As the creators of IMM, the Integrated Modelling Method, they have crafted a series of five groundbreaking books on creating Business Architectures for enterprises of all types and sizes, that are globally recognized. These books cover the topics of Requirements Gathering, Business Function Architecture Modeling, Data Architecture Modeling, Business Process Modeling, Business Procedure Modeling, and Information Flow Modeling.

Starting April 2023, their comprehensive collection of IMM books will be available worldwide. Immerse yourself in their powerful insights, whether you prefer the convenience of an eBook from Kindle or the tangible experience of a paperback from Amazon. Stay tuned for exact publishing dates.

For more information, simply reach out via email at support@integrated-modeling.com. Prepare to embark on a transformative journey with John Owens and Pam Walton, where proficiency and success are within your grasp.

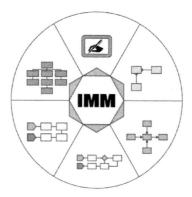

20.   Please Leave a Positive Review

We would love to know about your experience of reading this book.

If you had a **POSITIVE EXPERIENCE** with the book, then please share this with others by leaving a **POSITIVE REVIEW** on Kindle or Amazon.

If you found anything in it that you think we could improve, then please tell us about by sending an email to:

support@integrated-modeling-method.com

We would love to hear from you.

Thank you.

Pam & John

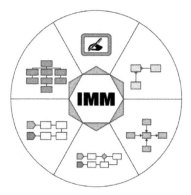

21. Glossary

This glossary contains definitions for all the elements of the **Business Architecture Models** of IMM, listed alphabetically. These models are Business Function Models, Business Process Models, Data Architecture Models, Business Procedure Models, Information Flow Models.

Where a definition contains a term that is defined elsewhere in the glossary it appears in **bold italic**.

Term	Description
Alphanumeric	This is the term used to denote that a **Data Entity Attribute** can contain all standard alphabetic and numeric characters. Although alphanumeric attributes can contain numeric characters they should **NOT** be thought of as numbers to be mathematically manipulated. If such manipulation is required, then the attribute should be defined as **numeric**.
Analysis and Extraction	This is the activity of analyzing all the materials collected during the **Requirements Gathering** stage of a **Business Improvement Project** and identifying and extracting **Business Functions** or **Data Entities** from them.
Analysis Stage	This is the stage of a **Business Improvement Project**, usually one to build a new software system, where the Enterprise is analyzed and modeled. The purpose of this analysis and modeling is to enable a system to be designed, built, and implemented that will support the effective execution of the **Business Functions** of the **Enterprise**.
AND Connector	This is where two or more flows in a **Business Process** from separate **Process Steps** (**Business Functions**) are merged into one flow before entering another **Business Process Step**.
Atomic Business Function	A **Business Function** at the bottom level of a **Business Function Hierarchy**. It is a Business Function with no **Child Business Functions**.
Attribute	A term commonly used to refer to **Data Entity Attributes**.
Business Aim	Some goal that a business wishes to achieve, for example, "Become the largest supplier of accountancy software in the UK." See also **Business Objective**.
Business Architecture Model	The term used to refer to a set of models built to represent a particular aspect of the Enterprise activities of an enterprise. In IMM these models include **Business Function Model**, **Business Process Model**, **Business Procedure Model**, **Data Architecture Model**, and **Information Flow Model**.
Business Champion	A person from within the Enterprise who plays an active part in a business improvement or systems development project whose key role is to "champion" the improvement within the Enterprise.
Business Function	A **Business Function** - also called a Function - is an activity or set of activities that a business must perform to meet its **Business Aims** and **Business Objectives** and continue in existence.

Term	Description
Business Function Decomposition	This is the term used to describe splitting *Business Functions* on the *Business Function Hierarchy* into lower-level *Business Functions*.
Business Function Description	A written description, in plain English, of what a *Business Function* is meant to do.
Business Function Hierarchy	The structuring of *Business Functions* into a hierarchical format with a *Root Business Function* at the top, *Grouping Business Functions* below that and *Atomic Business Functions* or *Elementary Business Functions* at the bottom.
Business Function Logic	A formal structured definition of what a *Business Function* does, using structured English, flowcharts, formulae, tables, etc. This would be an expansion of the *Business Function Description*.
Business Function Name	A short unique, succinct name for a *Business Function* that encapsulates the objective of that *Business Function*.
Business Function Objective	A concise statement of the purpose of a *Business Function*, i.e., what it is meant to achieve.
Business Improvement Project	Any project that is carried out with the intention of improving the performance of some aspect of an *Enterprise*. This improvement could take several forms, such as, structure, communications, conditions, systems, technology, etc..
Business Objective	A measurable *Business Aim*. For example, if the *Business Aim* for the *Enterprise* was "Become the largest supplier of accountancy software in the UK," then making this measurable by adding, say, "within three years" would change it to a *Business Objective*. The acronym *SMART* is a useful way to ensure that a *Business Objective* is properly and fully defined. Each objective should be *Specific*, *Measurable*, *Achievable*, *Realistic* and *Trackable*

Term	Description
Business Procedure	A **Business Procedure** is a set of steps to follow to perform a **Business Function** or a **Business Process** in line with current business practices, standards, and policies. **Example:** The Business Procedure to follow to perform the **Business Function** "Charge Customers for Products and Services Supplied" might be as follows: • Collect signed delivery notes from Distribution Supervisor • Check that delivery date is in the current financial month, if it is not, then file the delivery note in the "Pending" tray. • Create a new invoice in the invoicing system. • Enter details of the goods and services supplied. • Enter any extraordinary charges or rebates (such as rebates for pallets) • "Post" invoice to the ledger using F10 key. • Stamp delivery note as "processed" adding your initials and the date. • File delivery notes • Print invoices • Sort invoices by customer • Post (send) invoice to customer. Both businesspeople, and analysts often mistake **Business Procedures** for **Business Processes**.
Business Process	A **Business Process** – also commonly called a process – describes the order of execution of **Business Functions** in response to a specific **trigger** to achieve a **Preferred** or **Non-Preferred Outcome**.
Business Process Description	A description, in plain English, of what a Business Process does, what it includes and what it excludes. It is an expansion of the **Business Process Objective**.
Business Process Diagram	A diagram visually depicting a **Business Process**.
Business Process Flow	A term that refers to the order in which **Business Functions** are carried out in a **Business Process**.
Business Process Name	A unique name for a **Business Process** that succinctly encapsulates the objective of the Business Process.
Business Process Objective	A definition of what a **Business Process** is intended to achieve. This objective should align to the **Preferred Outcome** for the **Business Process**.
Business Process Step	A single step in a **Business Process**. Business Process steps are **ALWAYS** **Business Functions** taken from the bottom level of the **Business Function Hierarchy**, being either **Atomic Business Functions** or **Elementary Business Functions**.

Term	Description
Business Requirements	A term commonly used to refer to what a business needs or requires a *Business Improvement Project* to achieve. The term is too general to be useful and needs to be stated in quite specific terms, such as, "Business Functions to be supported," "performance requirements," "security needs," etc.
Business Sponsor	A person from within the *Enterprise* (usually an Executive or Senior Manager) who provides the budget and political drive to bring about the successful execution of a *Business Improvement Project*.
Candidate Business Function	Any phrase found when analyzing gathered *Business Requirements,* which <u>contains a verb</u> that represents an action or activity conducted as part of the business operation of an *Enterprise*. All such verb phrases are 'potential' or *Candidate Business Functions*.
Candidate Data Entity	Any noun contained in an *interview transcript*, *Business Function* name or flow on an *Information Flow Diagram* is a *candidate data entity* and should be included in the list of *Candidate Data Entities* that is built as part of the *Data Extraction Stage* of *Data Architecture Modeling*. When consolidated, the items in this list will turn out to be: • *True data entities* • *Attributes* of entities • *Occurrences* of entities • *Subtypes* of entities • *Synonyms* for entities
CASE Tool	**CASE** stands for "Computer Aided Systems Engineering." The term "CASE Tool" refers to a computer application which is designed to aid in the analysis and modeling of *Enterprises* and the design and construction of systems to support these operations of these *Enterprises*.
Chat Bot	
Child Business Function	Any *Business Function* in a *Business Function Hierarchy* grouped under a *Grouping Business Function*. All *Grouping Business Functions* can also be referred to as a *Parent Business Functions* because they have "children."
Consolidated List of Business Functions	The final list of *Candidate Business Functions* after all *Business Mechanisms* and duplications have been removed.
Critical Success Factor	A *Critical Success Factor (CSF)* is something that must occur in a project or in a business activity for it to be deemed successful. For example: • A *CSF* for a business activity might be that the response time to customer queries is reduced from 15 minutes to 5 minutes within three months. • A *CSF* for a project might be that the old accounting system can be switched off by the end of the financial year.

Term	Description
Data	A value in a particular format is called a datum. However, this singular form is now seldom used, having been superseded with the more familiar plural form, **Data**. Examples of items of data are: **Datum** **Description** 1 Integer to one significant figure. red Character string, three characters in length, lower case 3.9 Number with two significant digits and one place of decimals. 22 Oct 22 Date with numeric day number, first three characters of the month name (initial letter capitalized) and last two digits of the year.
Data Architecture Model	The full definition of the **data entities** and the structure they require to provide an **Enterprise** with the **Information** it requires to effectively execute its **Business Functions**. A complete **Data Architecture Model** will include: • A **Data Structure Diagram** • **Data Entity** definitions, volumes, synonyms, etc. • **Data Attribute** definitions and formats. • **Relationship** definitions • **Data Entity** and **Attribute** usage by **Business Functions, Business Departments** and **Automated Systems.**
Data Entity	A data entity, normally called an "entity," is anything (whether real or abstract) of significance to the Enterprise about which information must be known or held to support the **Business Functions**. Typical entities for a company might be "Customer," "Product," "Sales Transaction." Data is always either created or transformed by **Business Functions**. **Data is ONLY of SIGNIFICANCE to an Enterprise if it can be turned into INFORMATION that supports the execution of Business Functions.**
Data Entity Attribute	**Data Entity Attributes** describe, classify, qualify, or quantify **Data Entities**. Every **Data Entity Attribute** has a name and a **format**, for example: • Age: Number (2) • Description: Character (75) • Name: Character (25) • Weight: Number (4,2) **Data Entity Attributes** are commonly referred to simply as **Attributes**.

Term	Description
Data Extraction Process	The process of identifying and extracting *Candidate Data Entities* from *interview transcripts*, *Business Functions*, or *Information Flow Diagrams* as these are all *Candidate Data Entities.*
Data Flow Diagram	A diagram used in traditional business analysis, normally referred to as a **DFD**, showing the flow of data between *Business Functions*, *external entities*, and *data stores*. DFD's have been superseded in IMM by *information flow diagrams*.
Data Format	This refers to the format in which data is held by *Data Entity Attributes*. For example, the entity **Part** might have the following attributes and formats: **Attribute** **Format** Name Alphanumeric 35 characters in length – the abbreviation for this would be "Char (35)". Weight Number with four significant digits and two places of decimals – abbreviated to Num (4,2).
Data Store	A symbol on a *Data Flow Diagram (DFD)* representing an existing or planned means for storing *data*, usually a *Database*. **DFDs** are not used in IMM as they have many structural flaws that break the rules of good analysis.
Data Structure	A description of all the *Data Entities* in an *Enterprise* and the *relationships* between them.
Data Structure Diagram	A diagram displaying the *Data Entities* of an *Enterprise* and the relationships between them. A *Data Structure Diagram* is a major component of a *Data Architecture Model*.
Data Type	This refers to the type of *data* that a *Data Entity Attribute* can hold. The main *data types* are *alphanumeric*, *numeric*, *integer* and *date*.
Dependency	A term used (but not in IMM) to describe the association between two *Business Functions* on a *Business Process Diagram*.
Design Stage	This is the stage of a systems development project that follows the analysis stage and precedes the build stage. It is a vital stage in developing quality automated information systems. It is here that the system to be built is specified in physical detail. This specification, or "design," can be checked against the *Business Models* created during the analysis stage to ensure that it will properly support these models before the system is built.
DFD	See *Data Flow Diagram*.
Direct Form	This is the statement of an association between two objects, either in a *Business Process Model* or on a *Data Structure Diagram*, based on the order in which the objects appear. See also *Reverse Form*.

Term	Description
Elementary Business Function	This is a **Business Function** which, once begun, must be completed or, if not completed, must be undone. If there is a **VALID** intermediate stage for the **Business Function**, then it is **NOT** Elementary. At the end of the analysis stage of a systems development, **ALL** bottom level **Business Functions** on the **Business Function Hierarchy** ought to be **Elementary Business Functions**.
Enterprise	This is a generic name used in IMM to refer to businesses, organizations, local government departments, educational institutes, etc. that need to operate as a structured entity in order achieve some defined objective.
Entity	See **Data Entity**.
Entity Relationship Diagram	A diagram showing **Data Entities** and the relationships between them, normally referred to as an **ERD**. This diagram in IMM is called a **Data Structure Diagram**.
ERD	See **Entity Relationship Diagram**.
Event	A happening of significance to an **Enterprise** to which it must respond. There are two classes of **Event**: • **Triggers:** these are events to which the Enterprise must respond by starting up a **Business Function** or a **Business Process**. • **Outcomes:** these are events that arise as the result of the completion of a **Business Function** or **Business Process**.
External Entity	This is an element on an **Information Flow Diagram** representing an object outside the Enterprise, for example, Customer, Government, Supplier, to which **Information** flows or from which **Information** is received.
Focal Business Function	A **Business Function**, usually an **Elementary Business Function**, drawn at the center of an **Information Flow Diagram**. All **Data Flows** on the diagram are shown going to or from the **Focal Business Function**.
Function	See **Business Function**.
Grouping Business Function	This is a **Business Function** on a **Business Function Hierarchy** whose purpose it is to group lower-level **Business Functions** in a meaningful way.
Handoff	This is a term used when a business department passes control of a **Business Process** or **Business Procedure** to another department or to a third party outside the **Enterprise**. The term can be used in reverse when the other department or external party passes control back to the original department.
IFD	See **Information Flow Diagram.**
IMM	The **Integrated Modeling Method**.

Term	Description
Information	**Data** on its own has little meaning. For example, K3P3 is a **datum**, but what is it? Is it a cipher in a secret code, a foreign car registration or instructions in a knitting pattern (Knit 3, Purl 3)? Data in a context is Information. **Data is ONLY of SIGNIFICANCE to an Enterprise if it can be turned into INFORMATION that supports the execution of Business Functions.**
Information Flow Diagram	A diagram showing how **Information** flows from one **Business Function** to another or from a Business Function to a third party outside the **Enterprise**. In IMM all information flows are drawn between **Atomic Business Functions** or between **Elementary Business Functions**, whichever are at the bottom of the **Business Function Model**, at this point in time.
Instance of an Entity	If a business has a **Data Entity** called <u>Employee</u>, real life examples of this **Data Entity** might be the employees Fred Jones, John Thomson, and Karen Donnelly. Such real-life examples are referred to as **instances** or **occurrences** of the **Data Entity** <u>Employee</u>.
Integer	This term is used to denote that a **Data Entity Attribute** is a whole number (no decimal places) that can be mathematically manipulated. The convention allows the size of the integer to be specified as well, for example **Int (6)** denotes that the integer has six significant digits. If the number is required to have decimal places the attribute should be defined as being **numeric**.
Internal Trigger	An **Event** that occurs inside the enterprise to which it must respond by initiating either a **Business Function** or **Business Process**.
Intersection Entity	A **Data Entity** that resolves a **many to many relationship** between two **Data Entities**.
Interview Transcript	A typed or written copy of what was said at an analysis interview.
Key	A term often incorrectly applied to the **Unique Identifier** of a **Data Entity**. Keys (primary keys, unique keys, foreign keys) are not part of **Business Modeling** but of **Systems Design**. So, this term should **NOT** be used in **Business Modeling**.
Key Performance Indicator	A measure by which a **Business Function** is measured in terms of performing well or badly.
Leaf Business Function	Another name for an **Atomic Business Function**.
Loop, Looping	A **loop** in a **Business Process** is where control is passed back to a **Business Function** that has previously been executed in the **Business Process** for it to be executed again, to arrive at a desired state.

Term	Description
Many to Many Relationship	A *relationship* between two *Data Entities* that can have many *occurrences* of each *Data Entity* related to each other.
Business Mechanism	A *Business Mechanism* is how a *Business Function* is physically performed. For example, the Business Function "Bill Customers for Products and Services Supplied" might be executed by either of the following Business Mechanisms: • Print and post an invoice. • Electronic Data Interchange (EDI) In EDI, the computer of the supplier communicates directly with the computer of the customer and delivers an "electronic invoice."
Non-Preferred Outcome	This is a desirable but non-preferred outcome to a *Business Process*. It is where the Enterprise would desire a Business Process to stop if the *Preferred Outcome* cannot be attained.
Numeric	This term is used to denote that a *Data* A*ttribute* is a number that can be mathematically manipulated. The convention allows the size of the number to be specified as well, for example Num (6,2) denotes that the number has six significant digits with two decimal places. See also *Integer*.
Occurrence	This refers to an *occurrence* of a *Data Entity*. "John Smith" could be an occurrence of the *Data Entity* Employee; "England" would be an occurrence of the *Data Entity* Country. An occurrence of a *Data Entity* is also known as an **Instance** of a *Data Entity*.
Outcome	See *Preferred Outcome* and *Non-Preferred Outcome*.
Parent Business Function	A *Business Function* in a *Business Function hierarchy* that has other *Business Functions* hanging beneath it. The *Business Functions* hanging beneath the parent Business Function are called *Child Business Functions*.
Performance Indicator	See *Key Performance Indicator*
Precedence	A definition of what *Business Functions* must come before (precede) and follow (succeed) another *Business Function* in a *Business Process.*
Preferred Outcome	The objective that a *Business Process* is intended to achieve. If the *preferred outcome* cannot be achieved, then a predefined *non-preferred outcome* should be achieved instead.

Term	Description
Primary Key	The rules for **Relational Databases** state that **ALL** rows in a **table** must have a unique key and that this unique key cannot be null. This unique key is called the **Primary Key**. The term "primary key" or "key" is often **INCORRECTLY** used when referring to the **unique identifier** of a **data entity** and also confused with a **QUACK**.
Process	See **Business Process**.
QUACK	**Q**uick **U**nique **A**lternative **C**ode or **K**ey. A useful short way of referring to something, usually a product, in an **Enterprise**, e.g., PIPS could be the 'Personal Insurance Plan for Students.' **QUACKS** are often mistakenly used as **Unique Identifiers**.
Recursion	Another name for **looping** in a **Business Process**.
Recursive Relationship	When a **Data Entity** in a **Data Structure Diagram** is related to itself the **relationship** is referred to as a **Recursive Relationship**.
Relationship	A formal definition of the association between two **Data Entities**. Relationships are always two way so, if entity A is related to entity B, then entity B is related to entity A.
Repository Based	This is a term used to describe **CASE tools** that are not just diagramming tools but that hold objects in a database for use whenever and wherever required. All good CASE tools are repository based. All repository-based CASE tools are not necessarily good!
Requirements	The term commonly used to refer to "what a business requires" from a **Business Improvement Project**. It is a term that is too vague to be meaningful and ought to be avoided. See **business requirements**.
Requirements Gathering	This refers to a set of activities carried out at the beginning of a **Business Improvement Project** in order to find out from the Executive and Management of the **Enterprise** exactly what **The Business Improvement Project** is meant to achieve.
Reverse Form	This is the **STATEMENT** of an association between two objects, either in a **Business Process Model** or on a **Data Structure Model**, based on the **reverse** of the order in which the objects appear, emphasizing any constraints in this **reverse** direction. It is a powerful technique for checking the **Direct Form**. For example, if the direct form stated that "A starts after B" then the reverse form would state "B **CANNOT** start until A has finished."
Root Business Function	This is the **Business Function** at the top (paradoxically) of a **Business Function hierarchy**.

Term	Description
Service Level Agreement	This is an agreement made between an *Enterprise*, its customers, or suppliers or between enterprise departments on the time it should take to carry out specific tasks. It is an agreement between the parties of the "level of service" that one will provide to another. This "level of service" can be defined in terms of time or quality or both.
SLA	See *Service Level Agreement*.
Standard Business Life Cycle	The *Standard Business Life Cycle* says that, to operate properly and efficiently, an *Enterprise* should first **PLAN** what it is going to do, then **PERFORM** what it has planned, and **MONITOR** what it has done against the plan, re-planning to take account of variances. For this reason, all *Business Functions* that an *Enterprise* must perform can be classed as: **Plan:** Define what needs to be done, when it needs to be done and the resources needed to do **Perform:** Do what was planned to be done. **Monitor:** Check that what was done is what was planned and if not take appropriate action. The Standard *Business Life Cycle* is a useful structure to use at the top level of the *Business Function Hierarchy*.
Strategy Stage	The startup stage of a *Business Improvement Project* when all the major requirements for the project will be defined.
Subtype	This is a term used for a *Data Entity* that is like other entities in most respects but different in some significant detail. The "significant detail" might mean having an *attribute* or a *relationship* that is different. An example of sub types would be **Employee** and **Freelancer**. Both are types of <u>Worker</u> but are different in the attributes that would need to be held for both. In this example Worker would be a *Supertype Data Entity* that included <u>Employee</u> and <u>Freelancer</u> as *Subtype Data Entities*.
Supertype	This refers to a *Data Entity* that is subdivided into two or more *Subtypes*. For example, <u>Worker</u> would be a *Supertype Data Entity* if it had *Subtype Data Entities* of <u>Employee</u> and <u>Freelancer</u>.
SWOT Analysis	*SWOT analysis* identifies and defines the <u>S</u>trengths, <u>W</u>eaknesses, <u>O</u>pportunities and <u>T</u>hreats associated with all or part of an *Enterprise*, specific *Business Functions*, departments, or individuals, in fact for any item of significance. Good *SWOT Analysis* is essential to the success of *Business Improvement Projects* because it allows the *Enterprise* to build on strengths, eliminate weaknesses, capitalize on opportunities, be aware of and reduce threats.
Synonym	A *Data Entity* might be known by different names in various parts of the *Enterprise*. For example, Worker might be variously known as Employee, Recruit, Temp, Laborer, etc. If all these labels are the same thing (the "same" meaning that the information that needs to be known about them is the same) then each are *Synonyms.*

Term	Description
Trigger	An *Event* in an *Enterprise* that initiates the execution of a *Business Function* or a *Business Process.*
True Data Entity	During the *Data Extraction* stage of building a *Data Architecture Model*, many *Candidate Data Entities* will be identified and listed. When these have been consolidated and a unique name selected for each one, they change from being *Candidate Data Entities* to being **TRUE** *Data Entities*, or, simply, *Data Entities*.
Unique Identifier	The elements that make each *occurrence* of a *Data Entity* unique from a business and human perspective. These elements might be one or more *attributes*, one or more *relationships* or a combination of *attributes* and *relationships*. See also *QUACK*.
User	A person who uses a computer system. **This is one of the most misused terms in Business Improvement Projects** that is commonly used to refer to any member of the Enterprise who is **NOT** part of the project team. A user is "one of them" as opposed to "one of us." Good analysts avoid this term completely when referring to members of the Enterprise and use terms that are more accurate in that they refer to specific groups of people, for example, executives, department heads, process managers, senior managers, etc.
Workflow	This is the activity of scheduling, managing, and monitoring the tasks involved in *Business Procedures* in an *Enterprise* to ensure that they deliver in accordance with *SLA*'s, policy, objectives, or any other relevant business measures.